W9-AAJ-904

THE MURRAY HILL BIOGRAPHIES
ROBERT FROST

Photo by Doris Ulmann

ROBERT FR···

ROBERT FROST

A Study in Sensibility and Good Sense

By

GORHAM B. MUNSON

Author of "WALDO FRANK: A STUDY"

HASKELL HOUSE PUBLISHERS Ltd.

Publishers of Scarce Scholarly Books

NEW YORK, N. Y. 10012

1973

HASKELL HOUSE PUBLISHERS Ltd.

Publishers of Scarce Scholarly Books

280 LAFAYETTE STREET

NEW YORK, N. Y. 10012

Library of Congress Cataloging in Publication Data

Munson, Gorham Bert, 1896–1969.
  Robert Frost; a study in sensibility and good sense.

  Bibliography: p.
  1. Frost, Robert, 1874–1963.
PS3511.R94Z8 1973   811'.5'2   72–10857
ISBN 0–8383–0788–4

Printed in the United States of America

To
HART CRANE
in memory of many
enthusiastic conversa-
tions about poetry

CONTENTS

ROBERT FROST

A Study in Sensibility and Good Sense

ROBERT FROST

I. "THE GENERATIONS OF MEN"

*"But don't you think we sometimes make too much
Of the old stock? What counts is the ideals
And those will bear some keeping still about."*

NEW ENGLAND is our association with the
name of Frost, and we are no doubt surprised when told that it is a Scandinavian name.
Yet there are today many persons in Denmark
who hearing this sound uttered behind their backs
would turn with that sudden interest aroused by
the unexpected pronouncing of one's name. Certain of the remote ancestors of these Danish
Frosts may have roved into England in the ninth
century A.D., or it may have been Saxons bearing the name of Forst, which is the Saxon form
of Frost, who invaded England in the fifth century A.D. and founded the line of English Frosts.
In either case, the Frosts were settled there
before the Norman Conquest and the name had

begun to accrete sturdy Anglo-Saxon associations about its slightly harsh sound.

In 1135 Henry Frost, the probable ancestor of the American progenitor of one line of Frosts,* founded the Hospital of the Brothers of St. John the Evangelist at Cambridge, England, and this foundation became in 1509 St. John's College, for which reason it is said that "Henry Frost ought never to be forgot, who gave birth to so noted a seat of religion, and afterwards to one of the most renouned seats of learning in Europe."

The son of Henry Frost bore the name of the subject of this Study and wore a coat of arms which reads like a prophetic curio of the poetry of his namesake. "Argent. A chevron azure between two thistles slipped in chief, and a hind's head erased in base proper. Crest: a grey squirrel sejant, semée of estoiles sable, collared and chained or, and holding between the paws a hazel branch fructed also proper."

Until the early seventeenth century the Frost family spread deeper and deeper into the sub-soil of English life. Then came the migrations of the Puritans, crowded by unfavorable forces at home and drawn from afar by the promises of

* That of Elder Edmund Frost of Cambridge, Massachusetts.

New England. In an old piece of writing one can read:

"Nicholas, Marride Bertha Cadwalla,
Jan'y 1630   ffrom Tavistock, Devon
    Bertha Cadwalla, Borne ffeb'y ye 14th, 1610
    Aprill   Arrived in
Sailed for America   June, 1634, in ye year
    In ye Shipp Wulfrana, Alwin Wellborn, Master
    ffrom Plimouth, Devon."

It was this Nicholas Frost who founded the line of which Robert Frost is a representative of the ninth generation. In the interval New England incorporated itself into the tissue, blood and bone of these "generations of men" ultimately to become song from the lips of Robert Frost.

The history of the early generations of this line is threaded into the history of certain old villages in Maine—Kittery, Eliot, Wells, York— located close to the present New Hampshire border, and today there is an inscription on Ambush Rock where Major Charles Frost was slain, Frost's Hill is still known as such, and the Frost Garrison House, erected in 1733, is the only garrison house that remains in Old Kittery. Everett S. Stackpole, the patient chronicler of *Old Kittery and Her Families*, hints that a little mythological moss may have gathered about the early Frost settlers, and believes that Nicholas Frost was on the coast of Maine as early as 1632. He surmises that he returned to Tiverton, Devonshire, England, collected his wife and two sons, John and Charles, and came back to America in 1634.

Nicholas Frost appears to have landed at Little Harbor, now Rye, New Hampshire, and to have lived there for at least a year, since there is record of a daughter Anna being born there in April, 1635. Within the next two years he removed to the head of Sturgeon Creek, in what is now Eliot, Maine, where he made his home until his death in 1663.

His vicissitudes and achievements were of a typical pioneer character. He acquired a fairly large acreage of land, served as one of the first selectmen of Kittery, signed with his son a petition to Oliver Cromwell (signed with his mark, a combination of N and F, for this ancestor of a distinguished poet was illiterate), and lost his wife and fifteen year old daughter, Anna, to the Indians. It is said that they were captured on July 4, 1650 "and taken to a camp at the mouth of Sturgeon Creek. Nicholas and his son Charles were at York at the time, and on their return attempted to rescue them but were unsuccessful;

Charles, however, killed a chief and a brave. The next day Charles, his father and some of the neighbors went back to the camp but were too late. The camp was deserted, only the bodies of Bertha and Anna were found there. They were buried near the old Garrison." * Stackpole finds some of the details of this story scarcely credible, but it seems clearly a fact that Bertha Frost and her daughter were killed by the Indians.

Charles Frost, already mentioned several times in this narrative, became locally celebrated and until *North of Boston* was imported from England in 1915 was probably the most famous of the American Frosts.

He was noted as an Indian fighter, and bitterly hated by his foes who finally killed him from an ambush on July 4, 1697. The hatred of the Indians for him went to greater lengths: they opened his grave the night after the burial and carried the body to the top of Frost's hill where it was suspended upon a stake. The reason for this vengeance lay in an incident that occurred in September, 1676, following the close of King Philip's War, an incident that is sometimes described in the colonial and border war histories of our early settlers.

* *Frost Genealogy in Five Families* by Norman Seaver Frost.

The Pennacooks, some of the neighboring Abe-
nakis, and a number of "strange Indians" (alleged
to be King Philip's men) assembled, having been
given an express pledge of safety, at Dover, New
Hampshire, for a friendly conference with the
whites. A sham fight was instituted and using
this as a pretext the whites seized four hundred
Indians. Of these three hundred were sent to
Boston where a few were hanged and the rest sold
into slavery. It is said that Major Waldron and
Captain (later Major) Frost joined this stratagem with reluctance, but the Indians held them
responsible for what they reasonably deemed an
atrocious and treacherous deed, bided their time
and killed Major Waldron thirteen years later
and Major Frost twenty-one years after, causing
one Joseph Storer in Wells to write: "It hath
pleased God to take a way; Major Frost, the
Indians waylad him Last Sabbath day as he was
cominge whom from meeting at night; and killed
him and John Heards wife and Denes Downing
. . . it is a Great Loss to the Whole Province;
and Espesely to his fameley . . . mistress Frost
is very full of sory; and all her Children."

His death is said to have been the last English
blood shed in New England in King William's
War and inspired a memento in verse which runs:

"THE GENERATIONS OF MEN"

The last of that grand triumvirate,
Unflinching martyrs of a common fate,
Waldron and Plaisted and Frost, these three,
The flower of New England chivalry.

The descendants of this component of the flower of New England chivalry occupied themselves in divers ways but kept their home-roots within a radius of fifty miles of Portsmouth, New Hampshire. His son, the Hon. John Frost, married a sister of Sir William Pepperell who captured Louisburg in 1745 and himself served His Majesty for a time as Commander of the man-of-war *Edward*. Later he became a merchant of Newcastle, New Hampshire, and a member of the Governor's Council. His son, William, was also a merchant of Newcastle, but apparently not as conspicuous as his grandfather or father. The line recovers its warlike tinge in his son, Lieutenant William Frost, an officer in the Continental Army during the American Revolution and a resident of Andover, Massachusetts. The sixth generation gives us Samuel Abbot Frost, who remained in New Hampshire most of his life and was the father of four children, among them William Prescott Frost, the grandfather of Robert, who moved to Lawrence, Massachusetts.

For a time William Prescott Frost aspired to

be a well-dressed young blood, but New England
thrift and respectability erased these fashionable
yearnings and he became instead a saver of the
margins of his income and a local pillar of respectability. He wrested a competency from his
job as overseer in a Lawrence mill and was naturally somewhat baffled by the drifting and poetic
tendencies of his young grandson, probably never
more than when he proposed to Robert, then aged
eighteen, that he should take one year to try out
his poetry and then, if that did not meet with
success, why, there were plenty of other worthy
pursuits. The reply was: "Give me twenty
years!" And it was to be exactly twenty years
before *A Boy's Will* was published in London.

But for all his respectability there was a liberal
vein in William Prescott Frost: otherwise he
could not have tolerated the notions and conduct
of his wife. For she was one of the earliest
feminists in America. This lady, remembered as
one whose stateliness was enhanced by an habitual
nodding of the head as if with dignified resent-
ment against the ascendency of the male, decided
one day that house-work was not exclusively the
business of women and called for a division of
household tasks. And her husband acquiesced, so
that, turn and turn about, one performed the

services of the establishment whilst the other enjoyed leisure.

This couple had a son and a daughter, and named the boy William Prescott after the father. He was sent to Harvard, the first of the line to receive college training, and it was hoped that he would become a lawyer, a hope that his grandparents later cherished for Robert Frost. But William Prescott Frost, Jr., revolted against what seven generations of Frosts had assisted in forming: he revolted so strongly against New England that his flight ended only when he reached San Francisco.

But before recording that grimly energetic career, a pause is due, since "what counts is the ideals and those will bear some keeping still about," to ask concerning the congruity of Robert Frost with his ancestry. What is noticeable first of all in this stock is its closeness to the soil. It was given, not to wandering, but to settling, to making a sturdy fight with local conditions, to seeing matters through on the terms of the environment. That environment happened to be, in its wider sense, successively colonial America, the consolidation and growth of the United States, and the beginnings of the industrial era. In a smaller sense, it was New England and the family is dyed in the older qualities of both America and its small northeastern corner—hardihood, resistance, decency and kinship to the soil, to mention a few. One is tempted to make a second generalization. The way the Frosts trod was the middle road. In their family there is no touch of the eccentric or extravagant or fanatic. They were church-going, but not zealots of puritanism. They served in the army and navy when occasion pressed, but they were not soldiers of fortune. They were small business men and local officeholders, but made no unusual motions in either rôle. What stands out seems to be a temperamental conservatism, adapting itself to changes in history and environment, but never reactionary or radical—until we come upon a variant in the father of Robert Frost. But Robert Frost is heir to the progressive conservatism and the closeness to the locality of the forebears of his father.

II. "ONCE BY THE PACIFIC"

SHORTLY after the Civil War an immigrant ship from Scotland was coming up the Schuylkill River. It had taken weeks to cross the Atlantic and now it was close enough to be gaily bombarded by peaches thrown from the shore. The passengers caught the strange fruit in their hands and learned to eat it and the taste was welcome after so protracted a spell of ship's provisions.

There was a fifteen year old girl passenger from Edinburgh who did not take part in the pastime. She came of a lowland Scotch family, a family of seafarers: her father, a sea captain, had been lost at sea and so also had her brother. Bred to patience, she now sat quietly watching. But one of the men came over and dropped the peach he had caught into her lap. "You should eat it," he explained, and she replied, gazing at the fruit, "It's too bonnie to eat."

This Scotch girl was on her way to Columbus, Ohio, to live with an uncle in business there. A few years later she came to Lewiston, Pennsylvania, to teach school. And here it was that Isabelle Moody encountered William Prescott Frost, Jr., on his rebound from New England. Young Frost had his eye on other projects of ambition, but for the time he too was a school teacher in Lewiston. They were married, and the husband went on to San Francisco to work on a Democratic newspaper, the *Bulletin*. A little later he wrote his wife that the windows of the newspaper office had been shot out but he was unharmed. The paper had, it seems, printed derogatory statements about some stock and those who were interested in it had resorted to gun play. Into this smoldering and sometimes violent community Isabelle Moody followed her husband and there on March 26, 1875, a son, christened Robert Lee Frost, was born.

The christening tells the story of the father's political sympathies. Too young to fight in the Civil War, the boy had been an intense copperhead and had meditated on somehow slipping South to join the Confederates. Now he was a States' Rights man and once he showed Robert a map of the United States and divided it into five nations into which he predicted the country would sometime split.

The father liked San Francisco. He liked the

spirit of plunging which diffused through the community and he was himself always playing the stock market. He liked to spend money liberally. And he liked the threat of grimness which one experienced by simply observing that men wore revolvers with the frequency New Yorkers today wear sticks.

One Sunday afternoon Robert and several other children were permitted to walk along the beach with his father and a few associates. A bottle was found and stopped up and tossed into the waves. Out came the revolvers of all the men and they fired at the floating target. It was no more uncommon than throwing stones.

One Christmas Eve Robert, his sister and his mother returned to their house quite late. They were about to prepare for bed when his mother asked Robert if he had locked the door. He answered that he had, but it at once became indisputable that he had not, for the door was heard to open without benefit of key and some-one, to their consternation, entered. Mrs. Frost rushed her children into a room, locked its door, shooed them under a table, and extracted a revolver from a drawer. "I'll shoot if you come further!" she spoke with a quaver. There was no answer, and she repeated her threat. Then

Mr. Frost's laugh was heard, relieving a tension that was likely often to seize San Franciscans of that period.

On the Fourth of July the plunging editor broke loose. It was his day and it was neither safe nor sane. An old fashioned celebrator, he made the greatest racket possible, set fire to out-houses and destroyed minor properties. He went to the limit on political celebrations, too. In politics or the stock market he would soon make a lucky stroke if he played hard enough. Then after success had burgeoned, he would take care of that consumption that threatened him. He would take a trip to "the Islands"; that is, to Hawaii, the favored resort of that time for consumptives. In the meantime he drank liquor to keep up his pace, he drank warm blood at the stockyards to alleviate the disease, and he did all the celebrating possible when his party triumphed. Robert was a celebrant too, riding, costumed, on floats in the big parades or trudging in torchlight processions until he was sent home to bed from weariness.

But the political ambitions yielded only small fruits. Mr. Frost did go as a delegate to one Democratic National Convention and he was city campaign manager in 1884 when Cleveland was elected President. He was defeated, however, when he ran for election as tax collector of San Francisco. In that campaign the boy Robert was his constant companion—his job was to visit the saloons with his father's campaign cards and to impale these on the ceiling by flinging upwards a card with a tack through it and a silver dollar beneath the tack which worked as a sort of flying mallet—and this, one fancies, remains to this day the most active participation in politics of Robert Frost.

In 1885 consumption won the contest for the body of William Prescott Frost and silenced its teeming hopes and plans, its explosive moods and tense restraints. His wife who had suffered for weeks at a time from his gloomy silences and his son who had suffered from his grim severities mourned for him—and found that his extravagance had led to letting his insurance lapse. It was necessary to return to the New England the dead man had hated, to seek refuge with Robert's grandparents in Lawrence.

So the little boy relinquished the tiny chicken farm he had started in the backyard at San Francisco and on the long ride sat beside his surviving parent, both sunk in memories of the grim dignity of the deceased, he who had never worn anything but a top hat, who had always been drily polite without the least ingratiation, and yet had been pathetic, too, since he had been *terrible* to himself. If anything planted tragedy in Robert Frost, it must have been, one surmises, the vision of his father, friend on the one hand of Buckley, the notorious blind boss of San Francisco, and on the other of Henry George with whom for a brief time he managed a single tax newspaper.

Perhaps from his father he acquired a certain recklessness of temperament, less extreme, but discernible in the drifting ways of his life: his father was energetically imprudent and the world, one knows, judges the son gently imprudent in the affairs of practical living. But the presence of the mother is also implied in the poetry. Her Scotch blood, transmitted, courses perhaps in the canny good sense, in the slightly oblique humor, and above all in the thriftiness of the poetic pro-ductions. She was herself an occasional versifier and reviewed books for her husband's newspaper. In religion she was a Swedenborgian, and these facts are sufficient to suggest that she probably awakened an emotional area in her son that the father left untouched, that area that was later to fructify into a new contribution to American poetry.

26

III. "A BOY'S WILL"

ROBERT and his sister had been trained by their father to no love of New England. Circumstance, however, had now deposited them among the despised children of this section, and for the first time they saw pennies. They made up a little game. First, they would hold up a nickel and say, "San Francisco!" Then they would exhibit a penny and scornfully pronounce, "Boston!" But this childish snobbism soon vanished as they became more at home in the East. Robert received the usual schooling and in high school clearly outstripped his class. He was apparently in full possession of valedictorian honors as graduation neared when a rival emerged coming rapidly forward from a lower class. The rival was a Lawrence girl, a descendant of the Whites of Acton who fought at Concord and of Peregrine White on the *Mayflower*. Elinor White was completing her high school course in two and a half years, thus catching up with Robert's class, and when the averages were computed it was found that she had tied him for

the honor of valedictorian.   It was decided, never-
theless, that Robert Frost should deliver the address, while on the graduation program the names
of Elinor Miriam White and Robert Frost should
appear together as holders of the office.   This
happened to forecast the future, for the boy and
girl, already friends, were married in October of
1895 and their names have ever since been joined)
in a union of singular idyllic beauty.

Another courtship was developing during the
same phase of Robert Frost's life which was also
to ripen into a lifelong devotion, and that was
the courting of the Muse of Poetry.) Before he
left San Francisco, he had begun a serial story.
It concerned the doings of a lost and forgotten
tribe living in a ravine no one of the outside world
knew about.   After he came east, he continued
this serial from time to time, filling in the details
of scenery and inhabitants.

Here we strike a master-image, one that con-
stantly recurs in Frost's life, for aside from the
varieties of it to be found in his poems—for example, in such lines as "Me for the hills where I
don't have to choose" and the first two stanzas
of *Into My Own*—the poet has confessed that
often he puts himself to sleep by dreaming of this
inaccessible and sometimes happy tribe defending

28

its canyon. One hopes that this recurrent and dominant image will not be subjected to the ingenious but suspect leaps to conclusions of the psycho-analysts. Better far the slower method of the behaviorist who is in closer accord with the commonsense of man which tells us that we do not thoroughly know people until we have seen them in many situations over a lengthy span of seasons.

When fourteen Robert Frost began to open books with a new zest. Hitherto he had been content to have his mother read to him and his favorite story had been *Tom Brown's School Days* which characteristically he had never finished—because he could not bear the thought that he had completed the tale. But now he adventured for himself among books. He read with eager responsiveness all of William Cullen Bryant and Edgar Allan Poe. He went on to Shelley's *Alastor* and Keats' *Endymion* but found them too much at the time for his interests and resources. Edward Rowland Sill and his Emersonianism was better adapted to his requirements, and Frost still preserves a mild respect for this obscured Connecticut poet who in his day carried the fruitage of New England culture to the far West.

The following year at the age of fifteen Frost

was himself trying out his hand at writing verse, and two years later composed *My Butterfly* which is one of the pieces in *A Boy's Will* and the earliest poem he has kept. The first stanza is quoted not only to reveal its superiority to the poetry of adolescence at large but to explain what followed its publication.

> Thine emulous fond flowers are dead, too,
> And the daft sun-assaulter, he
> That frighted thee so oft, is fled or dead:
> Save only me
> (Nor is it sad to thee!)
> There is none left to mourn thee in the fields.

The tentative submission of *My Butterfly* to the *Independent* had brought a prompt note of acceptance and a check for fifteen dollars. It happened that William Hays Ward, the editor, was a devout student of Sidney Lanier, a fact that explains his liking for the musical dexterity of this poem, but though he printed some of the subsequent poems Frost mailed him, he never liked another as well. They were not in the Lanier vein, and that was where a young poet should be working. But Frost was obdurate then as now in these concerns, and Ward gave him up.

So at seventeen Robert Frost was looking very much like the Frost of today. He was dipping into literature apparently without system but really reading for his own purposes as a nascent poet. He was assimilating New England and coming close to an essence of its oldest settlers in a girl who was to prove an ideal helpmate through the years of unrecognition that lay ahead. He was displaying literary talent well above the merely good for those of his years. And he was showing a certain "set" character and pertinacity in finding out his own direction in poetry. William Hays Ward tried to divert him and failed. Twenty odd years later in London Ezra Pound at once recognized this "set-ness" and did not try to instigate any changes.

IV. "THE ROAD NOT TAKEN"

FROM 1892 to 1900 life offered Robert Frost a variety of prospective roads to travel. He refused them all after short reflection and continued to be drawn toward the road he had already peered at as a youth in high school. It was the road on which he should have Love and Poetry as presiding deities.

At the age of twenty he married Elinor White. Her father was a retired Universalist clergyman and she had attended a Universalist college, St. Lawrence University. But in deference to the faith of Robert Frost's mother, they were married by a Swedenborgian minister.

Robert, too, had been away to college in 1892. It was Dartmouth: he went at his grandfather's behest: and he stayed only a few months. Interests in him were beginning to ripen and somehow the college did not touch these interests. That was all, and quietly he withdrew to become for a time a bobbin boy in a Lawrence mill.

But he had no ambition to work up in a mill. That, like college, was a road not taken. In his pocket he carried a volume of Shakespeare which he read during rest intervals in the mill.

Somewhat restless, undecided and drifting those days were for him, and perhaps they are best symbolized by a brief tramping tour which he made down South.

His mother was taking pupils in her little school in Lawrence and Robert instructed there for a while in Latin. Previously he had had a spell of making shoes. Finally, he was the reporter-editor of the Lawrence *Sentinel,* a weekly paper. Reporting, however, was against his temperament. One had to be active to get the news, active and prying into the reticences of people. Robert Frost, respecting his own reticences, respected those of others, and the occupation was extremely distasteful. More to his liking was a germinal "column" he inaugurated, one into which he could insert vignettes he had written: the picture of a ragged child coal-picker in a railroad yard, the picture of the stray eagle who lit on the top of the American flag-pole of the Lawrence Post Office until some hours later it was shot down to Frost's indignation.)

Marriage did not precipitate the problem of making a living. Making a living merely continued to be a sort of hazy actuality about which eventually something would be done. But as another preparatory step to meeting this problem, Robert again tried college, again backed up by his uncomprehending but sympathetic grandfather. This time it was Harvard in the year 1897, and in the same class was another poet whose work Frost was to like years later but whom he did not know at the time. The other poet was Wallace Stevens.

Frost picked up something for himself during the two years he stayed at Harvard. He improved his acquaintance with Latin and Greek and particularly enjoyed reading Greek with a young instructor named Babbitt who later went to Trinity College. The ancient classics were much to his liking and it was about this time that he found in Virgil's *Eclogues* and *Georgics* the nourishment his emotional constitution most craved. Philosophy lured him in a general way as it continues to lure him. Santayana gave a course which he recalls with pleasure in the "golden speech" and the "deliberate speed, majestic instancy" of the exposition of this brilliant thinker.

But despite all this, college could not hold him to the end. There was a man in Windham, New Hampshire, he had known in the interval between

"THE ROAD NOT TAKEN"

Dartmouth and Harvard, a man named Charley Hall, whose speech had a racy commonness, and the stimulus of this man's talks was greater than the correct speech of college instructors. On the basis of this homely, shrewd and living talk, could not poetry be written by a good listener? Frost deserted academic halls for his own peculiar university, a life close to the soil among soil-tinged folk, listening to their turns of thought and feeling and phrase.

Journalism, handicraft, teaching, factory work, college, all were to be roads not taken, and in 1900 his grandfather was still pondering, perhaps more than Robert, on what was to be the career of his grandson.

V. "NEW HAMPSHIRE"

GRANDFATHER FROST reached a decision that to American poetry at any rate was fortunate. With $1800 he purchased a farm at Derry, New Hampshire, for his grandson and thither Robert Frost transported his family in 1900. The family now numbered four: a son, Eliot, had been born in 1896, and a daughter, Lesley, in 1899. Eliot, however, died in the middle of 1900.

Derry, which is in the southeastern corner of New Hampshire almost on a line northward from Lawrence to Kingston, New Hampshire, an old birthplace of Frost's ancestors, was apparently the right locality for the nurturing of Robert Frost's bents. Like a true New England village it had its academy, Pinkerton Academy, standing on a hill with Derry Village spread out below it. A mile away from that was the comparatively recent "Depot" where most of the five thousand inhabitants lived. But there was a breakage of character between the village proper and the "Depot." The latter was developing, rapidly of course, along the lines of present-day industrial New England: it had several shoe factories and foretold in its little way a new and confused order of society. But Derry Village was then very much as it had been in 1880. Its families were conservative and regarded their religion and inherited culture very stolidly, entrenched in the feeling that twenty or thirty years ago the satisfactory elevation in religious thought and education had been achieved and now required only maintenance. It had its local small scale industries, founded upon Yankee inventiveness, particularly the Chase mill, a woodworking plant which among other specialties turned out in large quantities the wooden tags that nurserymen employ to identify their stock.

All this was right for Robert Frost: a settled rooted community, its life persisting in the presence of an enveloping alien and noisy industrialism which has not yet succeeded in totally smothering its vitality, and the academy on the hill as a sign, however inadequate, that culture should keep conservatism a little worried about the large questions of life lest conservatism fall into complacency. "I believe in tradition and accident and a bit of an idea bothering tradition," Frost once remarked years after the Derry period, and Derry itself appears to have been a living pattern of this traditionalism affected by accident and ideas.

Frost's small farm was a couple of miles "down the turnpike." Like scores of other farms in Rockingham county it was a farm out of which even a very experienced farmer would have had difficulty in extracting a living. For Frost it was a downhill dogged battle. The unprolific character of the soil was unfairly aided in its resistance to success on the tiller's part by the hay-fever which attacked Frost in the middle of August each year and made him wretched for two months. In addition, it was the child-bearing and rearing phase of his married life. A son, Carol, born in 1902, a daughter, Irma, in 1903, and another daughter, Marjorie, in 1905 naturally increased the strain of his struggle.* In spite of all that, there was a good deal of play, too: botanizing, making wood paths, inducting the children into outdoor life. His farming neighbors, probably correctly, did not approve of Frost's methods (he could be caught milking the cows at ten at night in order to sleep later in the morning) and the end of this venture came in

* Elinor Bettina was born on June 20, 1907, and died on June 21.

1905 when he drove up to the butcher's to make further purchases on credit. The fattish butcher came brusquely out on the porch of his store, cocked an appraising eye at Frost's horse and inquired, none too delicately, if anyone had a lien on it. Then Frost, with four children, a rundown farm, and a bundle of unpublished poems (including *Black Cottage* which he had just written) on his hands, decided to apply for a position at Pinkerton Academy.)

If the farm had not grudgingly yielded him a living, it had done something else; it had toughened his respect for nature, it had disciplined him by its immalleability to aught but extremely hard labor. It put, in short, a fibrous quality in his living which has been expressed in the poetry.

It was almost literally with a poem that Robert Frost secured his position at Pinkerton. The incident was this: he had been invited to read a poem before the Men's Club of the Central Congregational Church at Derry. The reading aroused the interest of the Pinkerton trustees, among them, John C. Chase, the head of the mill; and the pastor of the church, Reverend Charles Merriam, used his influence in crystallizing this interest into an offer. And so Robert Frost came to worry and modify the traditional state of affairs at Pinkerton Academy during the years 1906 to 1911.

The reports of eye-witnesses have a superior validity in biography as well as in courts of law, and the author of this study is grateful to Mr. John Bartlett of Boulder, Colorado, for the privilege of utilizing portions of his letter on this period in Robert Frost's life. Mr. Bartlett wrote:

"I joined the class of 1910 in the fall of 1907, being rated then as a member of the Junior Middle Class. Pinkerton had a student body of one hundred and twenty or thereabouts, and its equipment consisted of a modern brick building on a hill-top and facing to the east, and a little lower on the hill the 'old academy' of wood, well preserved and painted white.

"There were several fine old teachers, excellent representatives of the school that believed that thoroughness and hard work were the beginning and the conclusion of the educational process. Great store was set by Latin which was taught by George W. Bingham, the stern and aged principal, and by Greek in which Mary Parsons, maiden member of a distinguished Derry Village (and New Hampshire, too) family, gave instruction.

"The faculty was true to the good old Pinkerton tradition. The Academy had been founded in the first years of the nineteenth century and dedicated to the development of cultured Christian character. Old rules governing the student body were still in effect. Card playing, for example, was forbidden, and for a boy to escort a girl to and from an entertainment was still a technical violation of 'requirements.' There were compulsory study hours and compulsory attendance at church. Students must be in their homes at seven p.m. and not leave thereafter except on Friday evening when grace was extended to ten p.m. and Sunday evening when the students were expected to attend church services. Once a week the principal called the roll of the assembled student body and each student reported his record of the week, thus: 'All the requirements,' 'One exception, excused,' 'Two exceptions.'

"Most of the students came from homes within a radius of fifteen miles. A great many were from farm families, while Derry 'Depot' sent the children of factory workers. An Academy-owned dormitory housed the majority of the few boarding students.

"I am sure that when I entered the Academy there was much faculty hostility to Frost, and

even among the older students there was some
also.) I recall that the submission to Frost as
the English teacher of all prepared papers in an
inter-class debate between Junior Middlers and
Seniors was objected to by the Senior team, a
grossly offensive act meriting disciplinary rebuke,
but such did not follow. (And I believe that there
were certain members of the faculty who had
toward the new English teacher almost a personal
animosity.)

"Frost came as the representative of new
things, and there was collision. He did not ar-
rive at the Academy in time to participate in the
morning chapel exercises; he had no classroom;
he defied the Pinkerton tradition in the infor-
mality of his presence and the free-and-easy way
he handled his classes. The fact that he had no
college degree would, for a portion of the faculty,
keep him forever outside the circle. He was
younger than nearly all the others. A dozen
things made him an 'outsider.' He looked it and
acted it.)

"The old order of things at Pinkerton went
quickly. A new principal, Ernest L. Silver (later
principal of the New Hampshire State Normal
School), came in 1909. There were new teachers
and new subjects—agriculture, domestic science,

and this and that. Pinkerton in brief time was doing a lot of catching up. (I believe that Frost's success with his English classes had a great deal to do with the rapidity and completeness of this change.)

"No greater departure from traditional Pinkerton teaching methods could be conceived than those of Robert Frost. A boy of sixteen or seventeen isn't aware in respect to much of a teacher's pedagogy beyond knowing whether it pleases him or not. But, looking back, I believe I know the first great difference between Frost and the other teachers. He had far greater interest in the individual student. He had a way of manifesting this, of asking questions and of making observations in a few words, all the while getting closer to the boy in question. It was not a professional self conscious thing, but a desire from Frost's heart to get closer and learn more.)

"A new member of one of his classes, I had handed in a single short theme. Late one afternoon as a group of boys were passing a football about on the athletic field, Frost came up. He was a frequent figure on the athletic field and sometimes he would take off his coat and 'make a bluff,' as the boys put it, at playing. This afternoon he happened to come near me. He asked

43

several questions concerning the Pawtuckaway Mountains where the 'Devil's Den' about which I had written was located. I answered them awkwardly: I was a shy boy. In a matter-of-fact way he observed that I was a fellow who had ideas.

"That was all there was to the conversation, for a spinning ball came my way, but I can still see Frost and the fall mud and the football bucking machine and the boys on that afternoon. He seemed to show in this conversation several hundred times the interest in me that other teachers had.

"He really had this interest, I am sure, and it was not directed toward me alone, but toward all his students. He asked them personal questions, drew them out.

"In those days Frost was always asking questions of people. Not the mechanical questions of politeness, but questions that would get at things Frost was interested in . . . and he was interested in a great deal. If we took a winter walk toward Londonderry and met a logging team, which stopped as we came abreast, there would be a conversation right there. Frost would have the teamster talking about logging things and horses and wood roads and such matters. He talked with his students in somewhat the same

44

way. There was always something to be learned
from these New Englanders, and Frost learned it.

"And he was interested in the boy's problems
of individuality. Seemingly, he could like any
sort of boy. He might not win a boy in the first
few months of his contact with him, but nearly
always he won him in the end.

"The most excited boy over an English paper
I ever saw was Dave Griffith, the athlete of '10,
a magnificent halfback and sprinter. He had
written on a sport subject and had earned com-
mendation from Frost. Breaking the study hour
rule of the dormitory, Dave stealthily went from
room to room to announce grandly his accom-
plishment. Dave had a haughty disregard for
scholastic honors in general (few of which he
ever received), but he knew when he had something to be proud of.

"We had a boarding student in the Junior
class, Arthur Eastman, who was neither among
the scholars on one hand nor the athletes on the
other. Arthur suddenly was famous for a four-
line stanza which Frost was commending to his
classes. I believe the boy never again wrote a
verse which was praised. On the other hand, one
of the older students who turned out verse with
great abundance and prided himself on his ability

received no approval whatever. The school knew that Frost considered this student's verse of no merit.

"Frost's English classes were always 'easy' classes. Frost had none of the taskmaster's attitude, yet his classes did a great deal of work and covered fully as much ground as any ordinary class. Any feeling for literature displayed by a student was cultivated: any talent for writing was nursed along. A few in each class were gradually developed who could always be counted on for lively discussion. Very frequently departures from the regular routine were made. Often, for example, Frost, slumped down in his chair, would read to the class. And every time a new *Critic* was out, Frost would discuss it with his classes.

"The *Critic* was the student publication, and it was better than it had been for many years before Frost's engagement. He let the boys and girls run it largely themselves: faculty supervision of it was much less than formerly. There was a good deal of comradeship between Frost and the *Critic* staff. Unconventional things occurred . . . the *Critic* files may contain at least one poem the distinguished authorship of which is not generally known. I believe the *Critic* sometimes contained, because of his 'hands off' policy, things that he would not have passed for publication. But he knew that his policy was right and held to it.

"He was philosophical, too, when one of the honor members of the Senior class, given liberty in connection with his Commencement essay not in keeping with Pinkerton practice, read a paper at Graduation which was a wretched failure. This boy had not been required to submit his essay for faculty approval. And he messed the job, actually writing the final paragraphs two hours before he was due on the platform. Frost remarked later, 'It sounded as though you had read one book or article and then written your essay.' That was all that was ever said between us, and it was enough! Frost had divined the fact.

"Out of the English classes came during those years several plays coached by Frost. In one year I remember we had Marlowe's *Dr. Faustus,* Milton's *Comus* and Yeats' *The Land of Heart's Desire.* The plays were a success on both sides of the footlights. Frost liked to have his fun as much as any of the students, and the rehearsals brought us all together in a fine way. These plays were a new thing at Pinkerton. The Academy had presented several of Shakespeare's plays since the century came in but no cognizance of other drama had been taken.

"In 1909 the state began to be interested in Frost's classes. He talked at conventions, booked by Henry Morrison, the New Hampshire State Superintendent. And from time to time educators visited our classes. These convention talks were ordeals, and Frost always came back from them in a condition of exhaustion. Once he made an experiment before a talk given at Exeter, I believe. He put sharp pebbles in his shoes and walked about for hours, painfully, hoping that physical pain would alleviate the mental torture he was in. But it didn't!

"The student body was with him one hundred per cent as the fall term of 1909 opened. There was a new order of things in the school and Frost was recognized as a big figure.

"I do not recall just when it was that Frost first wrote a formula, famous with his classes, upon a Pinkerton blackboard. He put forward the following kinds of matter used for literary purposes:

Uncommon in experience—uncommon in writing.
Common in experience—common in writing.
Uncommon in experience—common in writing.
Common in experience—uncommon in writing.

The last was the kind of material to search for, he told us.

"We celebrated a football victory over our rival school, Sanborn Seminary, in November, 1909, with a supper provided by the new domestic science department. Frost was the hit of the evening with a string of verses he put on the blackboard. This was one:

> In the days of Captain John,
> Sanborn Sem had nothing on,
> Pinkerton, Pinkerton.

"A few of the boys spent considerable time with Frost out of school hours. I remember a walk over the turnpike to Manchester twelve miles away in the late afternoon, an hour spent in a bookstore, an oyster stew, and then a ride home on the electric railway. Our conversation on walks touched books only now and then. They might include reminiscences of Frost's early life, discussion of school affairs, aspects of farm life in New Hampshire, some current news happening of importance, and nearly anything else. If in passing a farmhouse the aroma of fried doughnuts came out to us, Frost might propose that we buy some. Down around the corner we might encounter a fern he hadn't seen since he was last in the Lake Willoughby region. And if darkness overtook us and it was a favorable night for observation, Frost would be sure to take at least five minutes to study the heavens and attempt to start our astronomical education.

"There was always an abundance of conversation, but almost never any argument. Frost never argued. He knew what he knew, and never had any interest in arguing about it. In the same way he was always willing to let others think what they wanted to think.

"He had a Woodrow Wilson sense of loyalty. I never knew a person who was more sensitive to slights, rebuffs and acts of unfriendliness than Frost or who seemed to carry the scar of them longer, and I have never met one whose loyalty was more thoroughly of the lasting kind.

"I remember how I came back to Derry late in 1910, having left college 'between two days,' defeated and defiant, meeting disapproval and condemnation. I was a boy getting hit by life and receiving no friendly overtures when I needed them most. Frost heard I was back and walked miles to see me and take me over the country roads for a talk. I remember how a few months later he speeded me on my way to British Columbia with a handshake and a look in the eye.

There was a book at that parting, Chesterton's *Heretics.* I read it three times on the way out. I remember letter after letter as I sought a way to fit in at Vancouver, and the frequent letters as I finally started in newspaper work. Letters all about me, my problems. That was what friendship meant to Robert Frost, help to the maximum when a boy needed it."

One year after John Bartlett graduated, the teacher who had impressed him so strongly also left Pinkerton. The principal, Mr. Silver, had been appointed head of the New Hampshire State Normal School at Plymouth, New Hampshire, and as often happens in such cases he wished to take the pick of his faculty with him. Frost went to Plymouth for the school year 1911-1912, and while there formed a friendship with a teacher in the high school, Sidney Cox, now assistant professor of English at Dartmouth and editor of various texts. Professor Cox has furnished certain notes on his memory of this year which, like those of Mr. Bartlett, merit first hand presentation and thanks.

"I met Robert Frost," says Professor Cox, "in the fall of 1911 at a Normal School dance where both of us were against the wall. The next day he came to the high school to ask me to go for a walk. I went, and when I reached home I had felt from that one talk, as I had never done before, what the real nature of poetry is. Scales had been gently lifted off my eyes. After that came many walks, and long casual whole-souled talks. Mr. Frost had no congenial colleagues with whom to walk, and for both of us it was the first, and as it turned out, the only year in Plymouth.

"I found that Mr. Frost was having exciting times teaching psychology, that he wasn't following any chart, but improvising his own courses, and having the girls read real books. He made me interested in Plato's *Republic* and Rousseau's *Emile* when he was in the midst of them with one of his classes. He sometimes mentioned a student who seemed exceptional, but he didn't suppose he was making any great discoveries.

"Perhaps it was on the walk at the end of which Mr. Frost treated me at the drug store to the delectable beverage of white grape juice that he first made me realize the absurdity of letting students write compositions on the adventures of a penny, and gave me a realizing sense of the distinction between unconditioned speculation and creative imagination. He didn't put it in any such deadly abstract terms as that. He told me that at Derry he had directed his students to write about what was 'common to experience but uncommon to expression.'

"Sometimes we talked incidentally about things I was likely to take up in class. I remember his praising Matthew Arnold's *Sohrab and Rustum*, and critically admiring the craftsmanship in Mark Twain's *The Jumping Frog*, Stevenson's *The Bottle Imp*, Hawthorne's *Mr. Higginbotham's Catastrophe*, and H. G. Wells' *The Country of the Blind*. He invariably made me see something new. I first learned of Whitman from him, and at the same time found out that he was what I should formerly have considered objectionable and, without the point being formulated, that it wouldn't do to dismiss him because my taboo was infringed.

"One particularly beautiful snowy walk took us through an evergreen aisle for miles, down to the Interval and so to the turnpike from Boston. On the way up that state road to Plymouth I remember something started us talking about sex behavior and instruction in sex hygiene. Mr. Frost was skeptical about the latter and said he thought perhaps reading Shakespeare was more likely to avert catastrophe than any amount of scientific talk. Another time I told him about the

53

jumpiness and over-earnestness of one of the woman teachers in high school who boarded where I did, and I was permanently convinced of the wisdom of his remark that what she needed was an emotional education through poetry. He was always interested in people and never spoke of anyone slightingly. On the other hand, he was keenly aware of shams and stupidities, and he was not tender toward them.

"Besides the walks, there were a number of unqualifiedly delightful evenings at his home in the little white house, which he shared with the temporarily bachelor principal. His was a poor man's living room, but there was a bookcase with a lot of attractive books, many of them thin volumes of poetry,—I remember his drawing my attention to the exquisite Mosher books,—and there were two or three comfortable chairs. On such evenings the children went to bed and we older ones got comfortable, and Mr. Frost read aloud, or we talked. I suppose two of my favorite plays will always be *Arms and the Man* by Shaw and the *Playboy of the Western World* by Synge because of hearing Mr. Frost read them. I don't know anyone who can do the Irish so well. One evening he read from Mr. Dooley.

"He had supervised a triumphant production

of one of Sheridan's plays at Derry, and he scorned the notion that good things were too exacting for school children. The State Superintendent had discovered that he was the best of the English teachers under his administration soon after Mr. Frost had been invited away from his farm. And the Principal of Pinkerton had found that he was wrong in assuming that this teacher was hardly the man to address a farmers' institute. Regardless of the effort it was to overcome his nervousness before a crowd, Mr. Frost had showed that he had something to say, and could say it well. He took a sly pleasure in surprising people who automatically underrated him because he didn't have a college degree.

"In early spring Mr. Frost, the principal of the Normal School, one of my fellow teachers in the high school and I went a little way north to a farm for a week-end. Our host and hostess seemed rather flashy and hard people, New Yorkers I think they were. The woman was particularly metallic and thick, like a successful vaudeville performer; and I was much impressed with the considerateness and attention with which Mr. Frost kept up a two-sided conversation with her. They agreed, I remember, on admiring the New York skyline from the harbor. We talked until late that night, and the next morning after break-fast we walked over the snow to a large maple sugar camp. The religious and other metaphorical use of the lamb has always, since that time, been affected by the memory of Mr. Frost's waving his hand back and forth within an inch of the eyes of the lady's cosset, and pointing out that it never batted its eyes. I was unaccountably downcast on the way back to Plymouth and mentioned my mood. Mr. Frost commented, 'It's well to have all kinds of feelings, for it's all kinds of a world.'

"Not long after that I had to assume the duties of baseball coach, and Mr. Frost's lifelong interest in baseball helped me. He often talked of players and teams, and once he taught me how to work the short throw to shortstop when there were runners on first and third, and so catch the man stealing home. He was interested in tennis, too, and taught me very clearly what he had recently learned about three different cuts to use in serving.

"I think his one time of attendance at church in Plymouth was so disturbing to his sensibilities that he had a religious motive for staying away."

It is clear from the notes of these two friends that this was the crystallizing period in Robert

Frost's life. He became during it certain of what he knew as a youth and as a matter of fact a great deal of his published verse was written during these years. He had formulated his central article for his private *ars poetica*—to give an uncommon expression to what was common in experience—and he was not to deviate from that in his future course. By adhering to this, he was very soon after the year at Plymouth destined to be discovered and recognized by the literary public, but essentially the rest of his life has been a prolongation of the Derry-Plymouth phase. The enthusiasm of his friends, Sidney Cox and John Bartlett, when multiplied to the enthusiasms of critics, poets and readers at large did not, that is to say, alter his habits or his aims or his quality. He has continued to do a little farming, some teaching and some writing just as he did between 1900 and 1912.

VI. "PAN WITH US"

"Pan came out of the woods one day."

IT is difficult to overestimate the aridity of the minds and feelings of poetry editors in the United States during those years when Robert Frost was writing and teaching and farming in New Hampshire. Not by his own wish did he remain practically unpublished, for once a year at least he made up packets of his verses and sent them to the editors of *Scribner's, Century,* the *Atlantic Monthly* and one or two others. Almost uniformly they came back: the few exceptions were the *Forum* and *Youth's Companion* whose editor, Mark de Wolfe Howe, stretched a point or two of his editorial policy to include them. But the market for poetry was extremely limited, and the story of the insensibility of those who ruled the market has already been sufficiently told. Yet looking back, one still is mildly surprised that their taste did not welcome Robert Frost's work. It *was* fresh work, but yet not too far beyond their canons, not like the verses of

Ezra Pound, for instance, who had impetuously denounced Hamilton Wright Mabie and voyaged to Spain.

Certainly, Frost was not a persistent and resourceful salesman for his poems, and perhaps the fault lay partly in him for his lateness in publication.

> No wonder poets sometimes have to *seem*
> So much more business-like than business men.
> Their wares are so much harder to get rid of.

Occasionally, he admits, he looked at the poetry printed in the magazines, felt distaste for its mediocrity and lack of tang, and felt likewise jealousy and envy of the author because after all he had been published. Yet his own pride prevented him from making any energetic plan for breaking through the editorial attitude toward his scripts.

After the year at Plymouth he concluded that it was to be "now or never" with him so far as the Muse was concerned. The ten year conditions on his farm had elapsed and he succeeded in selling it. Now he would set aside the next three or four years for complete devotion to poetry. But where?

John Bartlett was getting on well at Van-

couver, B. C., and in September, 1912, planned
to marry a Pinkerton girl out there. Frost hesi-
tated between going to Vancouver and going to
England, and corresponded with his former student on the problem. But in August he wrote
that it was to be England for him. A letter about
the cost of living from the British Consul in New
York and certain talk in the family about living
under a thatched roof had decided the matter:
he would spend his free time abroad. So he
sailed in September, 1912, and, as has been noted
before, Harriet Monroe's *Poetry: A Magazine
of Verse* first appeared in October, 1912. Frost
left his country just one month before the event
which is usually taken as the beginning of a new,
more enlivened and more extensive interest in
contemporary American verse, and he stepped
into England during a particularly hopeful and
exciting season in the arts.

England just before the war of 1914-1918 was
full of idealistic movements and a new era seemed
about to open its buds. There was an upper
crust of writers—Shaw, Wells, Bennett, Conrad,
Hudson, Carpenter, Galsworthy, Chesterton,
Cunninghame Grahame, Max Beerbohm—that
was distinguished enough or respected enough to
make it worth while to continue their work or

to resist it or to try to supplant them. There were coming up such figures as D. H. Lawrence, Compton Mackenzie, and Gilbert Cannan for Henry James to cast a keenly appraising eye upon. There were at least two brilliantly edited reviews—Ford Madox Hueffer's (now Ford) *English Review* and A. R. Orage's *The New Age* —which sought for new work and instigated new literary developments. There were the Irishmen across their Channel working up a little re-birth on their own. Ezra Pound was everywhere, fighting, initiating, infusing fresh vitality into poetry and poetry discussions. Wyndham Lewis was breaking bonds in painting and prose. Imagism and vorticism, the Bloomsbury groupings and the reactionary schools, all made the scene stirring and great things were expected. Then the war crashed in and the fragility of all the movements became sooner or later apparent. But that was two years after Frost arrived.

At first Frost was not aware of this metropolitan ferment. He repaired to *T. P.'s Weekly* which conducted a department of country walks and inquired for quiet places in the countryside where he wished to live. The conductor of this department was an ex-policeman (and therefore as becomes a London "bobbie" intelligent in giving directions) and Frost took a fancy to him. On his advice he settled in the little suburban town of Beaconsfield in Buckinghamshire.

One night Frost sat before his fire spreading out before him his poems and reading them over. As was his custom, a certain number were discarded. Of those that remained he pondered on making a selection that might form some sort of coherent book. He shuffled through them, arranged and rearranged, and gradually *A Boy's Will* came to birth. He had a book of manuscript but no publisher in mind.

In this pass he recalled his friend, the ex-policeman, and determined to ask his advice on a publisher for poetry! The former policeman was equal to the call. He suggested Elkin Matthews, but said that as a rule he required subsidized manuscripts. Frost objected to that, and his counsellor brought up the name of David Nutt. This appealed to Frost: he remembered that David Nutt had been Henley's publisher: and thither he went one afternoon only to be told that he could not see David Nutt that day, but if he called the next day he would be able to do so. Coming at the time directed, he was ushered into a private office for an interview with a lady in dark clothes who informed him she would speak

for David Nutt. Later he learned that David
Nutt had been deceased for several years, and
the lady was his widow, but at this time the whole
proceeding impressed him as mysterious.

Three days afterward he received a letter stating that the firm of David Nutt would publish
A Boy's Will. The long period of twenty years
of frustrated publication was almost closed, and
the first drops of the exhilaration England was
to give him had touched his lips.

More were to follow presently. Walking in
London one day he noticed that Harold Munro's
Poetry Book Shop was opening its doors that very
evening with a reception and reading. Although
uninvited, he walked in with the crowd that night
and sat on the stairs during the festivities. A
man sitting below remarked, "I see by your
shoes you are an American," and introduced himself as F. S. Flint. Frost confided to him his
engagement in writing poetry, and Flint asked if
he knew his countryman, Ezra Pound. Frost
had never heard of Pound and was promptly cau-
tioned not to betray that fact to Pound himself.

Flint must have spoken to Pound about the
new arrival, for shortly there came to Frost's
suburban home a post card bearing an address,

the name of Ezra Pound, and beneath it: "At home sometimes."

Some months later Frost called at Pound's address and happened to find him at home. Piqued at first because Frost had been so leisurely in responding to his card, Pound soon warmed to his rugged caller with the boyish face and when he learned that possibly proof sheets of *A Boy's Will* might now be secured at David Nutt's he insisted on going at once to the office. The proof sheets were ready, and the pair returned to Pound's studio. Frost was directed to occupy himself in some way while Pound turned immediately to reading the poems. Satisfied that here was sound poetry, Pound then dismissed his guest with the remark that he had a review to write, and in a short time the first salutation to *A Boy's Will* appeared in type over the distinguished name of Ezra Pound.

A Boy's Will was received quickly and warmly by the literary press: the general tenor can be felt from a quotation from the notice in the *Academy*. It said: "We have read every line with the amazement and delight which are too seldom evoked by books of modern verse." The poetry-reading public was lured.

Pound had a new "find" and he began to take

Frost here and there to luncheons, studios and
parties, and among the most delightful of the last
were the Tuesday evenings at T. E. Hulme's.
Frost was pleased and interested, but did not
change his stripe.

All the time his capital was decreasing, for
although he was now a "success" * in a moderate
way, he never succeeded in winning any royalty
statements from David Nutt. *A Boy's Will* had
appeared in 1913 and the following year the same
firm gladly brought out *North of Boston* which
was greeted by the *Times Literary Supplement*
with the statement that "poetry burns up out of
it, as when a faint wind breathes upon smoldering
embers," and there were more buyers. But only
a success of estimation for Frost. To eke out his
capital, he fell back upon farming and in the
winter of 1914 leased a small farm called Little
Iddens near Leadbury in Gloucestershire. His
near neighbors were Wilfrid Wilson Gibson and
Lascelles Abercrombie.

Gibson enjoyed joshing Frost about America.
It appeared that Gibson's poetry aroused various
people in America to write him letters of grati-
tude that sometimes began, "Dear Bro.," and
proceeded to give other signs in orthography and

* See Appendix A.

Bott

grammar of semi-literacy and raw taste. Frost himself now received his first letter from an American admirer. It was on stationery of high quality from a farm in Stowe, Vermont, called Four Winds Farm. The neat script merely informed him that the writer and her mother had enjoyed his poetry, and the signature was that of a lady named Holt. It was a publisher's wife, though Frost did not suspect the fact. But the letter did enable him to return triumphantly Gibson's joshing: he displayed it to him as an example of the way farmer's wives wrote in America as well as evidence of the kind of people who read *his* books.

Gibson has commemorated this delightful time in a poem entitled *The Golden Room* printed some time ago in the *Atlantic Monthly,* and for the sake of the picture the first two stanzas may well be quoted here.

Do you remember the still summer evening
When in the cosy cream-washed living-room
Of the Old Nailshop we all talked and laughed—
Our neighbors from the Gallows, Catherine
And Lascelles Abercrombie; Rupert Brooke;
Elinor and Robert Frost, living awhile
At Little Iddens, who'd brought over with them
Helen and Edward Thomas? In the lamplight
We talked and laughed, but for the most part listened

66

"PAN WITH US"

While Robert Frost kept on and on and on
In his slow New England fashion for our delight,
Holding us with shrewd turns and racy quips,
And the rare twinkle of his grave blue eyes.

We sat there in the lamplight while the day
Died from rose-latticed casements, and the plovers
Called over the low meadows till the owls
Answered them from the elms; we sat and talked—
Now a quick flash from Abercrombie, now
A murmured dry half-heard aside from Thomas,
Now a clear, laughing word from Brooke, and then
Again Frost's rich and ripe philosophy
That had the body and tang of good draught-cider
And poured as clear a stream.

Meanwhile the war was increasing its diabolical momentum and the arts in England were going under. Poets went to the front instead of to studios and review offices, and among them was Edward Thomas with whom Frost formed his most congenial friendship on English soil. Thomas had been a critic and author of several biographical studies and travel books. Frost fanned the critic's hitherto latent talent for writing poetry to a quiet blaze and the outcome was the volume, *Poems*, by Thomas in 1917, a volume that was gratefully dedicated to Robert Frost. Thomas was killed on Easter Monday in 1917 and Frost has commemorated both the poetry and his friend.

ROBERT FROST

You went to meet the shell's embrace of fire
On Vimy Ridge; and when you fell that day
The war seemed over more for you than me,
But now for me than you—the other way.

Two years before the death of Thomas, in March
of 1915, Frost had left England for America,
bringing with him the fifteen year old son of his
friend.

He had gone through years of non-recognition:
in a foreign land he had been exhilarated with a
modest success and the sympathetic praise of fellow poets: all had been engulfed in the horror
and sadness of the greatest war in our history:
and now Frost faced again the uncertainties of
America. There was a surprise awaiting him.

VII. "INTO MY OWN"

PASSING down a side street in New York as
he came away from the steamer which had
brought him back from England, Robert Frost's
eyes saw propped on a stand a magazine he had
never heard of. From curiosity he purchased it
at once: it was called *The New Republic*. Inside
he came upon a page appreciation of *North of
Boston* which was signed by Amy Lowell. But
more arresting still, the book appeared to be published by Henry Holt and Co. An American
publisher! He did not know he had one. This
seemed a good omen, and the following day Frost
called on the Holt company.

Yes, they had imported the sheets for three
hundred bound copies from David Nutt, and this
small order had been very quickly exhausted.
Now they would like to publish *North of Boston*
and *A Boy's Will* themselves, but David Nutt had
reserved all rights. It soon appeared, though,
that David Nutt had violated the agreement, and
Henry Holt won the legal right to bring out
Frost's books in America. In quick succession

they published *North of Boston* and *A Boy's Will* within that year, 1915.

Rapid sales followed. *North of Boston* eventually ran around twenty thousand copies, and the other books have done well, considering the market for poetry, though not nearly so well as the first.* The critics were exuberant: among them was Edward Garnett who contributed an influential article on Frost, since included in *Friday Nights,* to the *Atlantic Monthly.* Furthermore, public taste for a time appeared to have crystallized about such work as Frost's. The hour was right, for there was ripening a new

* Five printings of *North of Boston* were called for in its first year, and ten more have been needed since. Its sale has been phenomenal for a book of poetry, and in 1926 it even led the author's later books, though each of them has been steadily in demand ever since it appeared. *New Hampshire, A Poem with Notes and Grace Notes,* which was issued in 1923, comes next in popularity to *North of Boston,* requiring five large printings. This book won the Pulitzer Prize for that year, while one of the poems included in that volume, namely, *The Witch of Coos,* won the prize offered by *Poetry: A Magazine of Verse* in 1922. *Mountain Interval* has also required five printings, and the *Selected Poems* are now in their fourth printing.

In London *New Hampshire* has appeared under the imprint of Grant Richards, Ltd., and the *Selected Poems* under that of William Heinemann.

In addition to their regular editions, a de luxe volume of *North of Boston,* illustrated in line by James Chapin, appeared in 1919, and a de luxe edition of *New Hampshire,* with woodcuts by J. J. Lankes, who also decorated the regular edition, came out in 1923.

interest in contemporary American verse: the critics were enthusiastic: and the character of Frost's writing, at once novel and conservative, pleased all camps. A great many people agreed with Edward Garnett's opinions: "It seemed to me that this poet was destined to take a permanent place in American literature. . . . Surely a genuine New England voice, whatever be its literary debt to old-world English ancestry."

Recognition, long deferred, now heaped itself upon the quiet poet. A chapter in Amy Lowell's *Tendencies in Modern American Poetry* was given over to him and his work, Louis Untermeyer wrote a chapter on his verse in *A New Era in American Poetry*, Llewellyn Jones did likewise in *First Impressions*, Clement Wood in *Poets of America*, and it very shortly came to pass that no survey of the poetry of our decades was complete without a considerable discussion of this author. Waldo Frank in *Our America* introduced his passage on Frost by saying: "The poetry of Frost is of that excellent sort which it is hard to catalogue. It is lyrical. It is dramatic, since his books are—as he says—'of people.' It is philosophic, since the tales he tells trace conscious lines about the boundaries of life. Fully, it is poetry—and of New England."

ROBERT FROST

Frost found himself an advisory board member of the *Seven Arts* in 1916 and 1917, that gallant venture in behalf of our national arts directed by Waldo Frank, Van Wyck Brooks and James Oppenheim. And in the file of the *Seven Arts* there rests *The Way Out,* the one published play by Frost. Truly, he had scarcely tapped and all the doors of literary America suddenly opened to him.

He had come into his own, so far as eminence counts. In 1916 he was Phi Beta Kappa poet at one of the colleges he had neglected to graduate from, and he read at Harvard for the occasion the poem called *The Axe-Helve.* Since then there has been a shower of honors. In the early part of 1922 he was elected an honorary member of the International P.E.N. Club in the company of Thomas Hardy, Anatole France, Romain Rolland, Selma Lagerlof, and others of western world fame. This international honor was seconded in the same year by the local action of the Women's Clubs of Vermont in conferring on him the title of Poet Laureate of that state. Very quickly, too, his work has been incorporated in the English literature courses of foreign universities: at the Sorbonne study of Robert Frost's books is a requirement in the English teacher's course and

from the University of Montpellier, Jean Catel
has written, "We are going to study Frost as a
poet together with such recognized writers as
Shakespeare, Milton, Thackeray, etc." Lately
critical estimates of his poetry have appeared in
Italy.

But Robert Frost was not to be hurried.
Mountain Interval came out in 1916 and ab-
sorbed most of the balance of his unpublished
poems. Then a wait until 1923 when a *Selected
Poems* was brought out, and then *New Hampshire,* the first new book in seven years. It is now
four years since *New Hampshire* and Frost is still
unwilling to release another collection. "In a
year or two I suppose I'll have another book
ready," he says.

The tables have been changed since Derry
days, but he continues the pattern. Therefore, in
1915 he purchased a farm on a hill just outside of
Franconia, New Hampshire. In 1920 he moved
to Vermont where he had purchased a large farm
at South Shaftsbury in the district presided over
by that ardent Vermonter, Dorothy Canfield.
He is still the farmer and poet. And teacher,
too, for that element in him retains its energy.
From 1916 to 1919 he was a member of the
faculty of Amherst College, this poet without a

scholarly eminence in the orthodox sense, without a college diploma even (though now he holds honorary degrees from three institutions of higher learning), but he was encouraged to conduct classes in literature and philosophy in his own freehand way. In teaching literature he assumed that the conspicuous landmarks would be seen in other courses. He could therefore ramble in the lesser known regions of good writing, dwelling always in his informal presentation on the enjoyment of books and slyly encouraging honesty of initiative in writing.

Then President Burton of the University of Michigan called Frost to fill the new Fellowship in the Arts which he established in 1921. The appointment was for one year, but was extended to two, at the close of which Robert Bridges, the British Poet Laureate, was appointed Fellow for the following year. But in 1925, so welcome had Frost been on the Michigan campus, he was called back to Ann Arbor to hold a life fellowship in poetry founded entirely for him.

It was not long, however, before the magnetic pull of New England soil and the fact that two of his children had made their homes in the east drew him away from the attractive post at Michigan. He resigned and came back to the ruggedly lyrical Green Mountains of Vermont in 1926, with the plan of distributing his "teaching" efforts among several colleges.

Thus during the academic year, 1926-1927, Frost was "boarded around" by the various colleges who competed for his residence on the campus. He traveled about, to Wesleyan University for two weeks, to Åmherst for ten, to Michigan for a few weeks, to Dartmouth for a visit, and so on, mingling in each place with students and faculty, giving lectures and readings, consulting with literary aspirants, imparting a fresh emotional quality to the collegiate routine that is too usually strange to it. But it is unlikely that he will "tramp about" so much in another year, as Amherst claims his *presence* (Frost does his teaching by simply being what he is) for an entire term during the next collegiate year.

*   *   *

Imagine that you have been invited to be the guest of Robert Frost for a few days. Let the place be Amherst. He is staying there for a month or two in a house rented from a professor now on his sabbatical year. As you alight from your taxicab late in the afternoon, a well filled out man of good height steps on to the porch, and you are aware that the note this waiting per-

75

sonality strikes is quiet yet vivid. A large boned rugged frame, a strong neck, and poised on its full column a head so modeled that it gives the strength of the body a lyrical accentuation. This head has been described as a faun's and the eyes and mouth are sometimes said to have an elfin quality, and indeed it is true that one might think of faunishness and sly flitting elves in glancing at it. That is fanciful, though, and not really in correspondence with the sensitivity, the fluent gravity, the friendly lines of the countenance now welcoming you. The words and manner are simple: there is a trace of shyness which attests that the simplicity is not an affectation and yet there is also ease.

You enter and Mrs. Frost, quiet, sweet, intelligent and devoted, greets you. Talk begins, dinner is served. Mr. Frost has been out of touch with the centers of literary life. He asks questions, about the *Dial,* about William Carlos Williams, about that and this eddy in the literature of the day. Patently, he is out of it, he doesn't follow the magazines and supplements and current books with any assiduity, apparently he prefers to hear—in country fashion—from the lips of the people he meets what is going on.

After coffee, you settle down in the living room

for a long evening's talk, you playing alternately the crisp rôle of questioner and the respectful one of listener, and Frost "in his dry, sly, halting way," as Elizabeth Shepley Sergeant puts it in her vivid portrait of Frost, talks and ruminates, tells stories, offers critical notes, and speculates. The speculative note in his conversation is important, for it signifies that the growing ends of his mind and feelings still carry him on. There is no impending death here of sensibility or thinking, no dogmatism, in short, that closes off further possibilities of enlarging his experience.

Perhaps he speaks of his Indian-fighting ancestor, Major Charles Frost, and how for years he looked on him with a little disapproval as a black sheep in the family whom other people honored for his treacherous conduct at the Indian conference. Frost, you perceive, sympathizes with the Indians: he doesn't like unfair play. But lately he has learned that Major Frost objected to the stratagem and entered into it with great reluctance: he is glad to think a little better of the early settler.

He drifts into reminiscence of San Francisco days and that grim father of his. Sometimes his father would give him some change and commission him to bring back cigarettes. But on one

77

awful occasion the quarter slipped from his hand
as he was running to the store and fell into one
of the cracks of the board sidewalk then the prev-
alent style in San Francisco. In vain did his
small hands try to recover it, and passersby were
able to do no better. Frantic, he went to the
store, fearfully explained he had dropped his
money, and begged for a package of cigarettes.
Laughter from the clerk and the men standing
about. Nothing to do but return home in trepida-
tion and tell his mother. Father was working
in his study and by now no doubt impatient for
a smoke. His mother also stood in fear of father's anger, but in the present case she decided
that Robert must go in and tell of the loss. Only
first let them pray, mother and son, that Robert
should be let off easily. Then Robert went in
and reported. His father glanced up for a moment from something he was writing, said
brusquely, "Never mind," and turned back to
complete his sentence.

There was something deep between Frost and
his father. The man was mentally alert: he had
stood second in his class at Harvard and he had
been an associate of Henry George. He was am-
bitious, as his political activity reveals. And he
was, despite his consumption, strenuous, engaging

in long swims and once in a six day walking race with the champion, Dan O'Leary. He won that, too. O'Leary had sworn that he could give him a liberal handicap and then walk him down. When O'Leary failed to do so, he claimed that Frost's father had violated walking rules, but afterwards he became his friend. But above all —and this is the really deep bond—his father seems to have planted tragedy into his son's view of the world: so deeply did he do this that to this day his father's character excites a species of awesome regard in the son.

And now, in reply to a question, Frost is speaking of school days in Lawrence, of first adventures in reading poets, of meeting Elinor White who tied him for scholarship honors. And he points out how his grandfather, according to his light, loyally stood by him, how he sent him twice to college, backed him patiently in various endeavors to make a living, and finally gave him a farm—which he didn't succeed in managing expertly. "Never earned a cent, save from and through verse. But for my first twenty years at it I earned a total of two hundred dollars," * he remarks without bitterness.

* Quoted from *Fire Under the Andes* by Elizabeth Shepley Sergeant.

The poem that he read before the Men's Club of the Central Congregational Church at Derry, the poem that was so instrumental in landing for him his job at Pinkerton Academy, was, he tells you, *The Tuft of Flowers* in *A Boy's Will*. "Yes," he says with a smile to interpret the remark, *"The Tuft of Flowers* got me my first real job. Whole family owe their life to this poem and they'd better believe it." * *The Black Cottage, The House-Keeper,* and *The Death of the Hired Man* all date, he goes on to inform you, from 1905 before he joined the Pinkerton faculty, and he adds that "Virgil's *Eclogues* may have had something to do with them. . . . I first heard the voice from a printed page in a Virgilian *Eclogue* and *Hamlet*." *

The talk shifts the scene to London . . . the fooleries of Skipwith Cannéll and Ezra Pound . . . the jiu jitsu demonstration Pound made on Frost's person in a restaurant. . . . Pound and Frost invited to luncheon by two ladies, Pound disgusted by their shallow flow of talk on art, Pound rising, knocking his chair over as he did so, saying haughtily, "I leave these ladies to you,"

* Quoted from *Fire Under the Andes* by Elizabeth Shepley Sergeant.

departing to Frost's consternation. . . . Pound's challenge to Lascelles Abercrombie to fight a duel on the score that Abercrombie's articles were a public offense—and the amusing aftermath.

We return to America and Frost tells how editors now snatched for the opportunity to print the poems which previously for many years had been vainly offered to their magazines. And you lead him on to tell how liberal the colleges have been in their attitude toward his way of conducting classes—a curious chapter in modern education.

Frost goes on to speak of the people he knows: of Lincoln MacVeagh and Alfred Harcourt when they worked at Holt's, of Carl Sandburg's work and Louis Untermeyer's visits, of a professor at Amherst he admires because "he loves the classics and he is a *field* scientist." He expresses his doubts of the "bunko-sciences" (mostly sociological and psychological in character). He tells of a night spent with Paul Elmer More at Princeton. He inserts somewhere one of Padraic Colum's Irish stories. He relates an experience at Vassar College. He supplied his audience with broadsheets on which were printed several of the poems he would read during his lecture. At the close of the talk the roomful of girls avalanched

upon him to autograph the broadsheets. After
that he no longer considered it a good idea to
furnish his audiences with the poems he intended
to recite.

The family is mentioned. His son, Carol, and
one daughter, Irma, are married: the oldest
daughter, Lesley, runs a book-shop in Pittsfield
but now she is going around the world, managing
a bookstall on the liner: Marjorie has not been
well for some time.

It is past two now. One studies Frost's face
in the lamplight. His "skin and his rebellious
hair have now a fine harmony of tone, 'the grey of
the moss of walls,' a young and living greyness
that, like a delicate lichen, softens without hiding
the hard and eternal shape of the rock beneath." *
And while one studies him, he is perhaps telling
you of the friendship that existed between him
and Thomas Bird Mosher. Mosher early picked
out one of Frost's poems for affection and printed
it in his catalogue, and Frost saw him every so
often, saw the sad decline of this epicure who
drolly mourned the loss of his sense of taste and
in desperation had beefsteaks specially sent from
Boston to Portland and specially prepared by the

* Quoted from *Fire Under the Andes* by Elizabeth Shepley
Sergeant.

best cooks he could engage only to find them taste-
less for him. But never to the end, Frost reminds
you, did Mosher lose his fine taste for the blue
china poetry of the nineties. Or perhaps he tells
you of Aroldo Du Chêne who sculpted his
head, or of J. J. Lankes whose woodcuts so
appropriately join in mood with the text of *New
Hampshire*. Frost had admired the feeling for
New England landscape Lankes had revealed in
some woodcuts reproduced in the *Masses* and
the *Liberator*. And Lankes had admired Frost's
poetry and illustrated several of the poems for
his own enjoyment. Then poet and artist were
brought together by Carl Van Doren, then an
editor of the *Century*, in a fortunate collabora-
tion for which each, unknown to the other, was
already prepared.

Somehow the talk shifts again. "I believe,"
Frost is saying, "in what the Greeks called synecdoche: the philosophy of the part for the whole;
touching the hem of the goddess. All that an
artist needs is samples. Enough success to know
what money is like; enough love to know what
women are like." * Nature, he explains, does not
complete things. She is chaotic. Man must

* Quoted from *Fire Under the Andes* by Elizabeth Shepley
Sergeant.

finish and he does so by making a garden and building a wall. That garden is art. Wallace Stevens, he says, has made a formal garden with his poetry.

* "One of the real American poets of yesterday," he goes on to say, "was Longfellow. No, I am not being sarcastic. I mean it. It is the fashion nowadays to make fun of him. I come across this pose and attitude with people I meet socially, with men and women I meet in the classrooms of colleges. They laugh at his gentleness, at his lack of worldliness, at his detachment from the world and the meaning thereof. When and where has it been written that a poet must be a club-swinging warrior, a teller of barroom tales, a participant of unspeakable experiences? That, today, apparently is the stamp of poetic integrity. I hear people speak of men who are writing today, and their eyes light up with a deep glow of satisfaction when they can mention some putrid bit of gossip about them. 'He writes such lovely things,' they say, and in the next breath add, half worshipfully, 'He leads such a terrible life.' I can't see it. I can't see that a man must needs have his feet plowing through

* Quoted from an interview in the New York *Times*, October 21, 1923.

unhealthy mud in order to appreciate more fully the glowing splendor of the clouds. I can't see that a man must fill his soul with sick and miserable experiences, self-imposed and self-inflicted, and greatly enjoyed, before he can sit down and write a lyric of strange and compelling beauty. Inspiration doesn't lie in the mud; it lies in the clean and wholesome life of the ordinary man. Maybe I am wrong. Maybe there is something wrong with me. Maybe I haven't the power to feel, to appreciate and live the extremes of dank living and beautiful inspiration.

"Men have told me, and perhaps they are right, that I have no 'straddle.' That is the term they use. I have no straddle. That means that I cannot spread out far enough to live in filth and write in the treetops. I can't. Perhaps it is because I am so ordinary. I like the middle way, as I like to talk to the man who walks the middle way with me. I have given thought to this business of straddling, and there's always seemed to me to be something wrong with it, something tricky. I see a man riding two horses, one foot on the back of one horse, one foot on the other. One horse pulls one way, the other a second. His straddle is wide. Heaven help him, but it seems to me that before long it's going to hurt him.

85

It isn't the natural way, the normal way, the powerful way to ride. It's a trick.

"I am an ordinary man, I guess. That's what's the trouble with me. I like my school and I like my farm and I like people. Just ordinary, you see."

He pauses. "What I have said," he reflects, "sounds a little too moral. My point always is that a poet may live as vile a life as he pleases, but then his poetry ought to be of a vile beauty. I hate dis-integrity. I hope I have some range in the appreciation of beauty. I can see it all the way from exquisite through homely and mean even to vile. What I am unsympathetic with is a wide discrepancy between life and art."

The college clock strikes three. It is Frost's usual bedtime. Tomorrow he will be up around eleven, a student or two will call with some writings for him to read, at one o'clock we are to be driven to a farm house for a "real New England luncheon," later there will be a walk.

"Frost," Waldo Frank has remarked, "is not only a beautiful poet. He is a beautiful person."

VIII. "A SENSIBILITIST"

"I'm what is called a sensibilitist,
Or otherwise an environmentalist."

THE poetry of Robert Frost is of one piece with his life and even with his physical appearance. Like the latter, it makes the impression of solid substance from which mounts a lyric flame whose light confers meaning on the mass. And it resembles his life in that the extraordinary in the shape of event or experience is usually quite absent: the materials are restricted and common. "Common in experience: uncommon in writing" is the true formula for practically all of Frost's poetry.

Whence arises his distinction in expression? The answer must first be made in terms of sensibility. The art of Robert Frost is built upon the foundation of observation: it is the poetry of observation, an emotional response, lyrical, dramatic, humorous, tragic, to what he has seen and heard.

When I see birches bend to left and right
Across the lines of straighter, darker trees,

87

I like to think some boy's been swinging them.
But swinging doesn't bend them down to stay.
Ice storms do that.   Often you must have seen them
Loaded with ice a sunny winter morning
After a rain.   They click upon themselves
As the breeze rises, and turn many-colored
As the stir cracks and crazes their enamel.

This is the type of sheer observation that abounds
in Frost's works, and one reads line after line that
requires no help for vividness from specially con-
structed images or even from simile and metaphor which are in their turn composed of other
definitely observed things.

The temperament of Frost, as befits an observer, is passive and plastic, and his impression-
ability depends in the first place for its intensity
upon the keenness of his ear and his eye.   In fact,
his style can almost be entirely explained by saying that he is a remarkably close listener and a
very sharp see-er.

Take his versification.   What is it but a disciplined and ingrained habit of listening to the
tones of speech in New England from the time
he was fascinated by Charley Hall's talk back in
Windham to the present?   The poems, although
they adhere to the molds of blank verse and
rhymed lyrics, are "talk poems."   The feat has
been that of conforming living speech to metrical

forms by taking advantage of the flexibility inherent in all metrical forms, so that Llewellyn Jones, a conservative student of versification, is right when he says:

"Technically, it is the outstanding feature of all Mr. Frost's verse that he makes it speak in human tones. He has never written a line of free verse that does not scan—if the reader knows how to scan English verse as it should be scanned and not as Latin or Greek verse should be scanned. The reason some people have thought Mr. Frost's verse very licentiate and why others have said that he writes free verse is because he subordinates his metrical pattern to the cadences of human speech. His metrical ictus is always there but it is not always emphasized, and he is never afraid to let a logical or word accent come in a weak place metrically. His verse is at the opposite pole from that of Swinburne, who gallops to an anapaestic tune in a manner which is quite alien to human speech. On the other hand: 'I shan't be gone long.—You come too' is pure and unadulterated human speech which just happens to fit into the metrical scheme of the poem. Only, such a thing 'just happens' so often in Mr. Frost's work that we know that it does not just happen at all but is the work of an exceptionally sensitive and gifted poet. And indeed Mr. Frost is so sure of the natural speech-tones in his work that he says that no one who reads his verse naturally can read it wrong. But on the other hand those who read it with a preconceived notion in their minds of how a verse should scan often find it a little difficult."

Frost himself settled the matter when he said to Miss Sergeant:

"They call me a dialect poet. . . . Not so you'd notice it. It was never my aim to keep to any special speech unliterary, vernacular or slang. I lay down no law to myself there. What I have been after from the first, consciously and unconsciously, is tones of voice. I've wanted to write down certain brute throat noises so that no one could miss them in my sentences. I have been guilty of speaking of sentences as a mere notation for indicating them. I have counted on doubling the meaning of my sentences with them. They have been my observation and my subject matter.

"I know what I want to do most. I don't do it often enough. In *The Runaway* I added the moral at the end just for the pleasure of the aggrieved tone of voice. There are high spots in respect of vocal image in *Blueberries:*

"A SENSIBILITIST"

There *had* been some berries—but those were all gone.
He didn't say where they had been. He went on:
'I'm sure—I'm sure—as polite as could be.' "

It is plain to see why Frost calls himself an
"anti-vocabularian," for the speech materials he
attends to are limited in number of words. But
there is a gain here: the right limitation of vocabulary will produce honesty of vocabulary, will
insure, that is, some personal content in experience for the words one employs, and this match-
ing of vocabulary and personal experience gives
force.

If Frost's ear gives a natural life to his verse,
his eye gives it a clarity, a definiteness, a firm-
ness of outline that produces a strong feeling of
actuality. Edward Garnett in his essay on Frost
lifted out from his better known poems a number of images and held them toward the reader
for inspection of their purity and hardness. We
may take a recently published poem, *Once by the
Pacific,** with the same purpose in mind, the more
so as this poem lies on Frost's usual plane of ex-
cellence and is not quite among his best.

The shattered water made a misty din,
Great waves looked over others coming in,

* Published in the *New Republic,* December 29, 1926.

And thought of doing something to the shore
That water never did to land before.
The clouds were low and hairy in the skies
Like locks blown forward in the gleam of eyes.
You could not tell, and yet it looked as if
The sand was lucky in being backed by cliff,
The cliff in being backed by continent.
It looked as if a night of dark intent
Was coming, and not only a night, an age.
Someone had better be prepared for rage.
There would be more than ocean water broken
Before God's last *Put out the light* was spoken.

Here we *see* rows of waves growing taller as we gaze out from the shore, and beyond above the fitfully glowing horizon the strands of clouds disordered by the wind. ("Great waves *looked over others* coming in. . . . The clouds were low and *hairy* Like *locks blown forward in the gleam of eyes*.") Already the scene is massive, and we are being prepared for the introduction of a cosmic word in the last line. The rest of the poem is devoted to heightening this anticipatory mood. We stand on the sand which is backed by a cliff which is backed by a continent: thus the scale of the struggle is enlarged to huge dimensions. The falling darkness of one night is similarly magnified: "not only a night, an age." And then the poem is ready to leave its symbolic frame altogether in the last two lines. "There would be more than ocean water broken Before God's last *Put out the light* was spoken."

It is this simplicity and coherence of imagery that creates the concreteness of Frost's vision. At the same time, grandiose though the theme is, the language is utterly like talk: the waves "thought of doing something to the shore that water never did to land before . . . you could not tell, and yet it looked as if the sand was lucky" . . . God will say, "Put out the light."

If Frost is thus faithful in the use of his own eyes and his own ears, it follows, since they cannot be universal in scope, that he will write about his own locality. He will be obliged to be American, New England, indigenous, to be an "environmentalist," to do things with the "native touch" Edward Garnett spoke of, because the very process of his writing poetry commits him to it.

But this is not all the story. The third conspicuous element in his style is his sense of situation, his sense of drama. This, too, has been often illustrated by the critics of Frost, and Edward Garnett has quoted in connection with it one of Goethe's offhand remarks: "A lively feeling of situations and an aptitude to describe them makes the poet." Frost has qualified in this way many times—in *The Death of the Hired Man,* in *Fear,* in *The Witch of Coos,* among many others. And he has given us one "straight" example of drama in the one act play, *A Way Out,* printed in the *Seven Arts.*

The scene is "a bachelor's kitchen bedroom in a farmhouse with a table spread for supper. Someone rattles the door-latch from outside. Asa Gorrill, in loose slippers, shuffles directly to the door and unbolts it. A stranger opens the door for himself and walks in" and takes a survey. "Huh," he says. "So this is what it's like. Seems to me you lock up early. What you afraid of?" And Asa replies in a piping drawl: " 'Fraid of nothing, because I ain't got nothing—nothing't anybody wants."

The situation has taken form at once: Asa Gorrill, the queer hermit, on the defensive, and the intruder, hurried, rudely questioning and commanding, mysterious. The dialog quickly develops both the characters and the situation. The stranger investigates the room and the old man's means as though perhaps his motive might be robbery—in case his suspicion of miserly hoardings finds evidence to go upon. He hints of violent action, of a necessity for hurry. He is aggressive, reckless, a factory hand in some sort of trouble. Asa trembles, wishes he were off, doesn't dare to resist, unwillingly answers the questions that build up a picture of his daily life— when he goes to market and what for, how he carries in his logs, what he believes in, what his history has been.

Then the stranger reveals he has committed a murder and is in flight. He was seen once during the day by a wagonload of women. He insists on donning some of the hermit's extra clothes and mimicking his behavior. The proposal is apparently that he hide here in the house and take turns with the hermit in "stretching his legs" abroad.

Dressed to resemble the old man, the murderer then drags Asa round and round in a game to get themselves dizzy. "And then when we're down," he says, "I want you should wait till you can see straight before you speak and try to tell which is which and which is t'other."

This is the high dramatic moment of the play as they fall moaning from their whirling and each accuses the other of the crime. The weak old man faints from terror in the excitement, the stranger clubs him with his fist and drags him out. The room is empty for a time.

A posse calls and the sham hermit fools it. Its members pass on. It is "a way out."

It will be noted that this play has both literary and theatrical form. The two are not the same: for instance, Eugene O'Neill, generally rated the best American playwright, often fails to produce a coincidence of what is visually effective with what is psychologically and dramatically determined. That Frost has done; the form stands up on the printed page as well as on the boards: the psychological springs of action are revealed: the writing is terse and necessary.

Needless to say, these elements of his style— the gift for tones of voice, the aptitude for concrete images, and the sense of the dramatic— would not suffice if they did not give rise to full-bodied, vital and corresponding emotions. Robert Frost is the type—the pure poet. The outline of his life has shown that he has all of the poet's traditional impracticality, though in his case there is no indulgence in utopian flights. Now, on the basis of his poems, we can add that he is emotionally centered, and the world is to him predominantly a source of emotion. It is his *sensibility,* and not ideas and his actions, that mostly strikes at his emotions, and the result is song inspired by *natural* objects which include, of course, people. Yet though his poetry is clearly not cerebral, neither is it thumpingly emotional. His personal make-up gives it its flavor—the humor and slyness, the sense of rural retreat, the friendliness. But to his intelligence goes the credit for its economy and restraint, its solidity and subtlety, for its bounding lines. Frost knows sufficiently what he is about in writing poetry to compose his own *ars poetica.*

"Imagery and after-imagery are about all there is to poetry. Synecdoche and synecdoche—My motto is that something must be left to God.

"In making a poem you have no right to think of anything but the subject matter. After making it, no right to boast of anything but the form.

"A poem must at least be as good as the prose it might have been. A poem is a box with a *set* or assortment of sentences that just fit together to fill it. You are rhyming sentences and phrases, not just words. They must go into it as unchanged in size and shape as the words.

"A straight crookedness is most to be desired in a stick or a line. Or a crooked straightness. An absolutely abandoned zig-zag that goes straight to the mark.

"Sometimes I have my doubts of words altogether and I ask myself what is the place of them.

97

They are worse than nothing unless they can do something, unless they amount to deeds as in ultimatums or battle-cries. They must be flat and final like the show-down in poker, from which there is no appeal. My definition of poetry (if I were forced to give one) would be this: words that have become deeds.

"All poetry is a reproduction of the tones of actual speech.

"There are two types of realists: the one who offers a good deal of dirt with his potato to show that it is a real one, and the one who is satisfied with the potato brushed clean. I'm inclined to be the second kind. To me, the thing that art does for life is to clean it, to strip it to form.

"A poem begins with a lump in the throat; a home-sickness or a love-sickness. It is a reaching-out toward expression; an effort to find fulfilment. A complete poem is one where an emotion has found its thought and the thought has found the words.

". . . . . . . the lines of a good helve
  Were native to the grain before the knife
  Expressed them, and its curves were no false curves
  Put on it from without. And there its strength lay
  For the hard work."

98

IX. "AGAINST THE WORLD IN GENERAL"

How about being a good Greek, for instance?
That course, they tell me, isn't offered this year.

SOME readers,* no doubt, were surprised when the poet told them in his last book, *New Hampshire:*

I may as well confess myself the author
Of several books against the world in general.

There had been no protest, no satire, no revolt to be noticed in his poetry. On the contrary, here was quietude, good humor and a certain manly acceptance of circumstance. Yet this author who never whines, who never seems savagely to resent the present state of affairs, this author considers himself to have been writing against the world in general! The surprise was salutary, for the shock directed attention to the implications of Frost's confession, the implications of his poetry *in toto*, and a study of these implications

* Page 99 to 110 appeared originally as part of an essay on Frost published in *The Saturday Review of Literature* for March 28, 1925. The text has now been slightly altered.

ROBERT FROST

will lead to the quite sudden realization that the purest classical poet of America today is Robert Frost.

With Frost in the field as a classicist, T. S. Eliot and Ezra Pound, conspicuous rivals for the title, begin to look like something else. Eliot's poetry, for example, has romantic elements: his sentimental melancholy and wistfulness, the dandyism and obfuscation that cut him off from a more general appeal. Pound likewise seems to be hewing no closer to a norm of thought, feeling and conduct: he does not appear to be making a bridge from the special to the general experience, to be achieving the "grandeur of generality": he is given up to the irritations and discomforts of a sensitive person. Yet a romanticist tinge does not make a romanticist and *au fond* Eliot and Pound are nearer to classicism than they are to romanticism. Still there is an important difference in kind between them and Robert Frost.

It is this: Pound and Eliot are in the main loyal to the principle of authority, whereas Frost depends entirely upon personal discovery. Pound and Eliot give allegiance to literary tradition as a governing body, seeking only to produce work that, while molded by tradition, still has suffi-

100

cient novelty of conception and style to alter somewhat the existing body of letters. Frost is unconcerned with such a theory of dictatorship, adjustment and modification: he does not set up a literary authority to serve. Like the intelligent Greek, he is simply by nature rather positive, critical and experimental. If he manifests the classical virtues, if he achieves a nature, an imitation of it, a probability and a decorum which can suggest those cultivated by the classical world, it is because he has discovered them in, through and by his own direct experience. In comparison with him, Eliot and Pound appear formalistic, and the distinction between them and Frost is the distinction between neo-classicism and classicism.

It is important to see that the classicism of Robert Frost has been evolved in a simplified world, the world of the New England farmer. Such a farmer has a settled routine of living dependent upon the seasons. He leads a village life in which most of the human factors at work have the appearance of being tangible and measurable. The intricacies of commerce and industry, the distress wrought by machines, the flow of vast crowds, the diversity of appeals of a great city, do not reach him. Churches are what they were, intellectual currents do not disturb, and science,

ROBERT FROST

arch-upsetter of former values, finds no opening
to intrude. Frost tells of a hugger-mugger
farmer who burnt his house in order to buy a
telescope with the insurance money. He gazed
with an unspoiled wonder at the heavens. But
for science at large the attitude is indifference.

> "You hear those hound-dogs sing on Moosilauke?
> Well, they remind me of the hue and cry
> We've heard against the Mid-Victorians
> And never rightly understood till Bryan
> Retired from politics and joined the chorus.
> The matter with the Mid-Victorians
> Seems to have been a man named John L. Darwin."
> "Go 'long," I said to him, he to his horse.

In Frost's New England then many of the com-
plex tormenting questions that have arisen since
the small city and agrarian communities of old
Greece have been lopped away from the problem
of living.

> "Me for the hills where I don't have to choose."

With this simplified world given, Frost has
built his art, as was pointed out in the preceding
chapter, upon the foundation of observation, and
it is by positive and critical observation of things
conceived as discrete that Frost has discovered
his Nature.

"AGAINST THE WORLD IN GENERAL"

The end reached by observation as a method, whether it is a poet or a scientist who employs it, is dualism,—that is, a set of axioms and laws founded on distinctions. The distinctions are based on appearances and both they and appearances are treated as reasonably final data. Of course, something inscrutable remains beyond, "something must be left to God," as Frost says, but the fundamental truth or error of dualism is not plumbed. At any rate, whether or not the real world is dualistic, certainly the apparent world is.

So in Frost's poetry we are consistently struck by his acceptance of the dualistic world and his actual contentment with his lot of joy and love "dashed with pain and weariness and fault." Nature we feel as a sort of friendly antagonist, dangerously strong sometimes, but on the whole a fair opponent. In combat with her one cannot laze or cheat: but honest struggle brings fair returns. Especially is the line between Nature and Man always present in Frost's mind, though never insisted upon. For example, he spends no time dilating on the aloofness or indifference of nature to man. Such a poem as *The Need for Being Versed in Country Things* illustrates very well the sense of demarcation between man and nature which Frost preserves, his acceptance of nature as lovely and fair, and his awareness of her unconcern for man's disasters. In this poem we hear of the burning of a farmhouse and the decay of its barn. The birds nest in the latter.

> Yet for them the lilac renewed its leaf,
> And the aged elm, though touched with fire;
> And the dry pump flung up an awkward arm;
> And the fence post carried a strand of wire.
>
> For them there was really nothing sad.
> But though they rejoiced in the nest they kept,
> One had to be versed in country things
> Not to believe the phoebes wept.

Frost's poetry contains no taint of the "pathetic fallacy" of the romanticist which in these days is almost sufficient ground for suspecting Frost's classical tendencies.

The man that Frost treats is situated in a tamed wilderness and is disciplined by it. In New Hampshire the mountains are not high enough, there is nothing extravagant or unduly wild about nature, nor are the people of Frost's poems grandiose or expansive. Their bodies have been contracted and hardened by sweating toil, their emotions are rock-like, and their minds achieve a good dogged horse sense.

"AGAINST THE WORLD IN GENERAL"

For art's sake one could wish them worse
Rather than better. How are we to write
The Russian novel in America
As long as life goes so unterribly?
There is the pinch from which our only outcry
In literature to date is heard to come.
We get what little misery we can
Out of not having cause for misery.
It makes the guild of novel writers sick
To be expected to be Dostoievskis
On nothing worse than too much luck and comfort.

*   *   *   *   *   *   *   *

It's Pollyanna now or death.
This, then, is the new freedom we hear tell of;
And very sensible. No state can build
A literature that shall at once be sound
And sad on a foundation of well-being.

Out of a settled social framework, an honest necessary struggle for existence, and a fair amount of well-being, something like a representative man can emerge. There are balances and checks to trim down his uniqueness while at the same time there is permitted a moderate scope for his emotional and reflective life. In such a state the acquisitive impulse gets no favoring head start and instead of haste we find reticence and deliberation characteristic.

Thus Frost discovers what Professor Irving Babbitt would call a sound model for imitation.

ROBERT FROST

Professor Babbitt has labored to show that imitation as the ancients understood it was a fresh and imaginative process. It is just so with Robert Frost. His choice of words, his rhymes, always escape the commonplace: we are awakened by the exact perceptions of a new discoverer. But the more important point is that this stirring-up is followed by a conviction of the naturalness or the obviousness of Frost's statements. Why, we murmur, has this not been said before? Again we are repeating Poe's useful test question for the workings of the imagination.

One cannot be certain just what content the term, the imagination, contains today. Modern psychology has cleared away some of the rank underbrush which has cluttered our view of the imagination, though it has planted other bushes to confuse us at the same time: but at least we habitually distinguish imagination from fancy. Perhaps by pure imagination we mean something not far from a total sweeping flash-like view taken by a human being at unusual moments. At any rate Frost's imagination is based on the view of a man who is using *more* of his equipment than most of the moderns do. The meaning is simply that Frost does not seem to write almost exclusively from one of three centers,—from the

intellect or the emotions or the instinctive center,
—but from a sort of rude partnership of all three.
The conditions of his erstwhile livelihood (farming) brought into at least partially coördinated
play his body and his emotions, and in addition
he is capable of thought. In this growth he is
again a parallel, though distant, to the ancient
writers, and gives a start to the speculation as to
how far the conditions of modern mechanized
life throw into disuse portions of the necessary
equipment of a fully aware human being. Certainly, Frost's lines give one more of an impression that a whole man is writing them than do the
sharply intellectualized or bubbling emotional
lines of most of his contemporaries.

The moot interpretation in the doctrine of
imitation has always been the meaning to be at-
tached to universals. One may rightly be skeptical as to the coincidence of the views of the
idealists with the original meaning of Aristotle.
But whether Aristotle is interpreted idealistically
or not, Frost's use of universals arising from a
welter of particulars is covered in the minimum
definition that could be offered. His poems,
Mending Wall and *The Grindstone*, are prime
examples: in these poems the particulars are viv-
idly and concretely seen and they can stand the

most rigid literal interpretation. Yet no less present and vivid in them is a wider significance or rather there are wider significances. Thus, among other things conveyed in *The Grindstone,* we are deeply aware that a sense of the inertia of nature has been induced. We are aware of the aching strain of making nature malleable and the tear and wear made on the straining human being by time. For readers of Frost it is not necessary to add that this creation of universal significance is accomplished directly without an atom of didacticism.

Although the doctrines of nature and imitation as exemplified in the works of Robert Frost have been so briefly dwelt upon, does it seem requisite to develop the contiguous statement that Frost is an observer of the law of probability and the law of measure or proportion or decorum? It is simply stating an easily recognizable fact which any reader may verify by going through Frost's writings that it is the probable sequence and not the improbable but possible sequence that he develops. He is a poet of the customary in man and nature, not the exploiter of the remarkably arresting and wonderful. Nor does his feeling for decorous proportion require argument beyond saying that he does not commit the mistake

of the neo-classicists who have been properly ac-
cused by Professor Babbitt of confusing the language of the nobility with the nobility of language. Frost's people are humble, but they speak
a language and utter feelings appropriate to
them: they are restrained by conventions which
are inherently worthy of respect, and the result
is decorum in the true sense.

The study of these considerations should explain why Frost declares that he has written
several books against the world in general. For
since Rousseau romanticism has been in the ascendency. A new conception of nature as impulse and temperament has supplanted the old
nature as a strict model, a "return to nature" has
come to mean "letting one's self go." For imi- a-
tion has been substituted the self-expression of
the spontaneous original genius, for the law of
probabilities has been exchanged the law of wonderful possibilities, and for decorum we have the
doctrine of expansiveness. Science has abetted
the growth of naturalistic emotionalism, and
neither humanism nor religion has been able to
stop the tide of writing designed for the expression of uniqueness rather than of generality.

Against this efflorescence of the interior world,
the neo-classicists have striven in vain, for their

position does not rest solidly enough upon experience and personal discovery. They have been debilitated by the blight of Scaliger's rhetorical question, why imitate nature when Virgil is a second nature?

Frost however quietly takes his place beside the antique Greeks and against the modern world. He proves that a species of classicism resting on personal discovery is still possible.

Pictorially, Frost's apartness from contemporary currents is striking. . . . He came on our literary scene, this intensified and intelligent and subtilized "ordinary man," in very queer company. There was Carl Sandburg with his love of the blur, his dreamy slothfulness, his drifting impressionism, there was Vachel Lindsay, sentimental, picturesque and declamatory, there was Amy Lowell, shallow and decorative, there was Edgar Lee Masters, protestant and disillusioned, and these were the poetic vanguard of Frost's generation. In the novel Theodore Dreiser was working up a public appetite for naturalism, and Sherwood Anderson, recoiling in disgust from American business life, was starting toward his present trust in objectless wandering and instinctive laughter. Romantics all, and so were the new critics, J. E. Spingarn with his gusty estheticism, H. L. Mencken, braying out his prejudices, and Van Wyck Brooks with his humanitarian approach. Frost came on with this troop, and they hailed him as a brother. He was contemporary with them in age and public appearance, and a mistake was made: it was taken for granted that he belonged in attitude and spirit and general aim to the so-called "new poetry."

Today the Middle Generation is beginning to recede whereas Robert Frost emerges more and more and as a poet differing at the root in substance, craft and direction from the romantic movement of the last decade. Where is his kinship in America? Not with that other New England poet of parts, Edwin Arlington Robinson, for Robinson exemplifies a withering and retrospective New England and Frost exemplifies the New England that is still sturdily alive. No, it is rather in the Eldest Generation in American letters that one finds a similar temper and approach to Frost's. One imagines that the elder critics, Paul Elmer More and Irving Babbitt, casting skeptical eyes over our literary life today, might single out Frost and say: "Here is a poet who has not succumbed to the 'law for thing': here is a poet who has not bleached himself with neoclassical dogma: here is a poet who sings afresh in the great classical tradition."

Ultimately More and Babbitt diverge, as More seeks to sustain the religious tradition of classicism and Babbitt to revitalize the humanistic tradition. It is the latter tradition that includes Robert Frost.

For speaking in terms of psychology rather than of literature, what distinguishes Frost is simply good sense. Good sense avoids extremes both in what it denies and in what it accepts. It does not, for instance, deny the bulky evidence of the senses and the man of good sense, therefore, will not accept the lies of idealism. The external world he will try to see and feel and otherwise sense as clearly and tangibly as he can: "the fact is the sweetest dream that labor knows." At the same time the man of good sense will not in his acceptance of the practical instinctive fact as such fly to an extremely narrow materialism and atheism. Something inscrutable and ordering very likely remains: there are overtones in the observer of the fact that he cannot ignore. Thus, he neither denies God nor the world: he accepts the latter as demonstrated and the former as probable or at least possible.

What he does trust is his own experience (having good sense he knows that there is nothing else to trust) and his own experience happens in Frost's case to be mediatory in character. Being intelligent, being deeply emotional, being obliged to make terms with practical life, the man of good sense casts up a rough balance of the three aspects of his life and travels, so far as he is permitted so to do, in the center of the highway.

A fair-minded description of a poet ought to be in itself a placement and therefore a criticism of that poet. If Frost's qualities pertain to good sense, we must not expect him to write on the religious level. In *The Trial By Existence,* one of the poems in *A Boy's Will,* he took up a religious theme, the gathering in heaven of the souls ready for birth, "the trial by existence named, the obscuration upon earth," and the conclusion reached is sensible. As Llewellyn Jones has stated it, it is "a recognition that suffering is always in terms of what we are, not an alien something hitting us by chance from without but somehow or other implicit in our very constitution." But *The Trial By Existence* is exceptional in theme and treatment in all of Frost's range.

Nor must we expect from Frost that rarest and most difficult of virtues that goes by the prosaic name of commonsense. Commonsense is a *com-*

munity of judgments, intellectual, emotional and practical, upon life. It is an exact balance demanding the utmost strenuousness to achieve and the perfection and harmony of our faculties. Good sense is a gift: commonsense must be deliberately arrived at, as witness the efforts of Socrates.

There are certain all-important questions which only the greatest literature raises and attempts to answer, and these questions it is not appropriate to ask of every poet. Frost makes no pretense of great inclusiveness and great profundities. The canniness of good sense forbids such rash over-reachings of one's self. But what we have always a right to demand is that the poet should be skilled in his craft, alive in his sensibility, and at least sensible in his conclusions. Robert Frost is all of these, and to those questions that it is proper to ask of him, those questions, that is, that are covered in his own experience, he returns always an answer in true currency equal to the demand.

His comprehensive answer is the *natural* (not romantic and not religious) vision of life, and it is natural in the sense that it is fitting to man *as he is*. "The poetry of a true real natural vision of life," said Goethe, "demands descriptive

"AGAINST THE WORLD IN GENERAL"

power of the highest degree, rendering a poet's
pictures so life-like that they become actualities
to every reader," and that is what Robert Frost,
man of good sense and fine sensibility, has succeeded in writing, and for that he will be treas-
ured in what we hope, against many odds at
present, will be the long and noble course of
American literature.

115

APPENDIX A

The following quotations are taken from a little leaflet distributed by David Nutt. Historically, the leaflet is interesting for showing the quick captivation of English critics by *North of Boston*. But more than that, the English writers appear to have succeeded better in stating the emotional character of Frost's verse than the Americans who have undertaken the same task.—G. B. M.

. . . A unique type of eclogue, homely, racy, and touched by a spirit that might, under other circumstances, have made pure lyric on the one hand or drama on the other. Within the space of a hundred lines or so of blank verse it would be hard to compress more rural character and relevant scenery; impossible, perhaps, to do so with less sense of compression and more lightness, unity and breadth. The language ranges from a never vulgar colloquialism to brief moments of heightened and intense simplicity. There are moments when the plain language and lack of violence make the unaffected verses look like prose, except that the sentences, if spoken aloud, are most felicitously true in rhythm to the emotion. Only at the end of the best pieces, such

117

ROBERT FROST

as *The Death of the Hired Man, Home Burial, The Black Cottage,* and *The Wood Pile,* do we realize that they are masterpieces of deep and mysterious tenderness.—*The English Review.*

. . . To start with, Mr. Frost is an American poet who noticeably stands out against tradition. . . . We find very little of the traditional manner of poetry in Mr. Frost's work; scarcely anything, indeed, save a peculiar adaption, in his usual form, of the pattern of blank verse. . . . It elaborates simile and metaphor scarcely more than good conversation does. It is apt to treat the familiar images and acts of ordinary life much as poetry is usually inclined to treat words—to put them, that is to say, into such positions of relationship that some unexpected virtue comes out of them; it is, in fact, poetry composed, as far as possible, in a language of things. . . . We have heard a great deal lately of the desirability of getting back again into touch with the living vigors of speech. This usually means matters of vocabulary and idiom; and Mr. Frost certainly makes a racy use of New England vernacular. But he goes further; he seems trying to capture and hold within metrical patterns the very tones of speech—the rise and fall, the stressed pauses and little hurries, of spoken language. The kind of metrical modulation to which we are most accustomed—the modulations intended for decorations or purely esthetic expressiveness—will scarcely be found in

his verses. But, instead, we have some novel in-
flections of metre which can only be designed to
reproduce in verse form the actual shape of the
sound of whole sentences. As a matter of tech-
nique, the attempt is extraordinarily interesting.
. . . Naturally, this technical preoccupation bears
strongly on the general form of Mr. Frost's
poetry. He uses almost entirely dialogue or
soliloquy; he must have somebody talking. We
might call these poems psychological idylls.
Within their downright knowledge, their vivid
observation, and (more important) their rich enjoyment of all kinds of practical life, within their
careful rendering into metre of customary speech,
the impulse is always psychological—to set up,
in some significant attitude, a character or a con-
flict of characters. The ability to do this can
turn a situation which is not very interesting at
first into something attractive, as when a rather
protracted discourse of two distant relations on
genealogy gradually merges into a shy, charming
conversation of lovers; or, in a more striking instance, when the rambling speech of an over-
tasked farmer's wife works up into a dreadful
suggestion of inherited lunacy. If, as we have
said, we cannot quarrel with this deliberate
method of exposition, it can scarcely be ques-
tioned that Mr. Frost is at his best when he can
dispense with these structural preliminaries as in
the admirable soliloquy of a farmer mending his
wall, or in the exquisite comedy of the professor

sharing his bedroom with a talkative newspaper-agent, or in the stark, formidable tragedy called *Home Burial*. Though it is difficult to state absolutely the essential quality of Mr. Frost's poetry, it is not difficult to suggest a comparison. When poetry changes by development rather than by rebellion, it is likely to return on itself. Poetry in Mr. Frost exhibits almost the identical desires and impulses we see in the "bucolic" poems of Theocritus.—*The Nation.*

. . . There is such a thing as vers libre, which is an excellent instrument for rendering the actual rhythm of speech. I am not in the least suggesting that Mr. Frost should write vers libre; I am only saying that it seems queer that he does not. There was Whitman—But Mr. Frost's achievement is much finer, much more near the ground, and much more national, in the true sense, than anything that Whitman gave the world. I guess he is afraid of the liberty of vers libre; to shackle himself probably throws him into the right frame of mind. It is another form of the New England conscience. . . . He does give you a very excellent, a very poetic, a very real sense of his meadows and woods and rocks and berries, and of night and of showers and of wildnesses—of an America that really matters far more than the land of endless trickery, make-believe, and lying and empty loquacity. That is the face that—Heaven knows why!—America seems to like to present to these parts of the

world; but those are the least desirable features.
Anyhow, Mr. Frost has called in on us to redress
the balance of that particular New World. . . .
He is not a remains of English culture grown
provincial and negligible. He is not, in fact, a
sentimentalist. Not to be a sentimentalist is to
be already half-way towards being a poet—and
Mr. Frost goes the other half-way as well, though
to describe what that other half is beats me. Here
is the little poem—rhymed for a change—in
which, as it were, he proffers his invitation to read
North of Boston.

THE PASTURE

I'm going out to clean the pasture spring;
I'll only stop to rake the leaves away—
And wait to watch the water clear, I may;
I shan't be gone long—You come too.

I'm going out to fetch the little calf
That's standing by the mother. It's so young
He totters when she licks it with her tongue.
I shan't be gone long—You come too.

Why is that beautiful and friendly and touching
and all sorts of things? I don't know. I suppose,
just because Mr. Frost is a poet.—Ford Madox
Hueffer in *The Outlook.*

This is an original book which will raise the
thrilling question, What is poetry? . . . Few
that read it through will have been as much

astonished by any American since Whitman.
. . . He has trusted his conviction that a man
will not easily write better than he speaks when
some matter has touched him deeply. . . .In
his first book, *A Boy's Will*, there is this piece,
entitled *Mowing*:—

There was never a sound beside the wood but one,
And that was my long scythe whispering to the ground.
What was it it whispered? I knew not well myself:
Perhaps it was something about the heat of the sun,
Something, perhaps, about the lack of sound,—
And that was why it whispered and did not speak.
It was no dream of the gift of idle hours,
Or easy gold at the hand of fay or elf:
Anything more than the truth would have seemed too
   weak
To the earnest love that laid the swale in rows,
Not without feeble-pointed spikes of flowers
(Pale orchises), and scared a bright green snake.
The fact is the sweetest dream that labor knows.
My long scythe whispered and left the hay to make.

Those last six lines do more to define Mr. Frost
than anything I can say. He never will have
"easy gold at the hand of fay or elf": he can
make fact "the sweetest dream." Naturally,
then, when his writing crystallizes, it is often in
a terse, plain phrase, such as the proverb, "Good
fences make good neighbors," or—

> Three foggy mornings and one rainy day
> Will rot the best birch fence a man can build;

or

APPENDIX A

> From the time when one is sick to death,
> One is alone, and he dies more alone;

or

> Pressed into service means pressed out of shape.

But even this kind of characteristic detail is very much less important than the main result, which is a richly homely thing beyond the grasp of any power except poetry. It is a beautiful achievement, and I think a unique one, as perfectly Mr. Frost's own as his vocabulary, the ordinary English speech of a man accustomed to poetry and philosophy, more colloquial and idiomatic than the ordinary man dares to use even in a letter, almost entirely lacking the emphatic hackneyed forms of journalists and other rhetoricians, and possessing a kind of healthy, natural delicacy like Wordsworth's, or at least Shelley's, rather than that of Keats'.—Edward Thomas in *The New Weekly*.

In its quiet and unsensational way, Mr. Robert Frost's *North of Boston* is the most challenging book of verse that has been published for some time. . . . Mr. Frost has turned the living speech of men and women into poetry. . . . To me it seems that *Home Burial* and *The Fear* are the most absolute achievements in the book; but that may only be because they come nearest to the kind of thing I wish to see done in poetry; and the other pieces in the book all contain not-

ROBERT FROST

able qualities, and qualities which have been too long absent from English verse. Mr. Frost has a keen, humorous sense of character. . . . Tales that might be mere anecdotes in the hands of another poet take on a universal significance, because of their native veracity and truth to local character.—Wilfrid Wilson Gibson in *The Bookman*.

APPENDIX B

BIBLIOGRAPHICAL

BOOKS BY ROBERT FROST

A Boy's Will. London: David Nutt. 1913
North of Boston. London: David Nutt. 1914
North of Boston. New York: Henry Holt. 1914
A Boy's Will. New York: Henry Holt. 1915
Mountain Interval. New York: Henry Holt.
   1916
Selected Poems. New York: Henry Holt. 1923
New Hampshire. New York: Henry Holt. 1923

PRINCIPAL ESSAYS ON ROBERT FROST

Amy Lowell: *Robert Frost* in *Tendencies in
   Modern American Poetry.*
Waldo Frank: pages 158-162 in *Our America.*
Louis Untermeyer: *Robert Frost* in *A New Era
   in American Poetry.*
Edward Garnett: *Robert Frost* in *Friday Nights.*
Clement Wood: *Robert Frost* in *Poets of
   America.*
Llewellyn Jones: *Robert Frost* in *First Impres-
   sions.*

ROBERT FROST

Elizabeth Shepley Sergeant: *Robert Frost* in *Fire Under the Andes.*

Percy H. Boynton: *Robert Frost* in *English Journal,* Oct., 1922.

G. R. Elliott: *The Neighborliness of Robert Frost* in the *Nation,* vol. cix, p. 713-715.

Carl Van Doren: *Quintessence and Subsoil* in the *Century,* February, 1923.

John Freeman: *Frost* in the *London Mercury,* vol. xiii, pages 176-187.

Charles Cestre: *Amy Lowell, Robert Frost and Edwin Arlington Robinson* in *Johns Hopkins Alumni Magazine,* vol. xiv, pages 363-388.

Jean Catel: *La Poesie americaine d'aujourd'hui* in the *Mercure de France,* March 15, 1920.

Albert Feuillerat: *Robert Frost* in *Revue des Deux Mondes,* tome xvii, pages 185-210.

APPENDIX C

ROBERT FROST ON EDUCATION

The following extracts are from a talk which Robert Frost gave at Wesleyan University in December, 1926. They were taken down in shorthand by a reporter for the *New Student* and thus preserve the exact verbal flavor of Frost's conversation as well as the best direct statement of his educational aim that I have encountered.— G. B. M.

"The freedom I'd like to give is the freedom I'd like to have. That is much harder than anything else in the world to get—it's the freedom of my material. You might define a school boy as one who could recite to you, if you started him talking, everything he read last night, in the order in which he read it. That's a school boy. That's just the opposite of what I mean by a free person. The person who has the freedom of his material is the person who puts two and two together, and the two and two are anywhere out of space and time, and brought together. One little thing mentioned, perhaps, reminds him of something he couldn't have thought of for twenty years. That's the kind of talk I'd rather give.

"I'd rather be perfectly free of my material—

reach down here in time and off there in space, and here's my two and two put together. Here's my idea, my thought. That's the freedom I'd like to give.

"It depends so much on the disconnection of things. There's too much sequence and logic all the time, of reciting what we learned over night. There's an attempt in the honor courses to get toward what I mean. I don't know what the honor courses will do toward it.

"I think what I'm after is free meditation. I don't think anybody gets to it when he's in anybody's company—only when his soul's alone. I do it when I wake up in the morning, when I'm starting an idea, and restarting. Sleep is probably a symbol of the interruption, the disconnection that I want in life. Your whole life can be so logical that it seems to me like a ball of hairs in the stomach of an angora cat. It should be broken up and interrupted, and then be brought together by likeness, free likeness.

"You might ask me this question: how am I going to find time? I would so run a course by self-withdrawal. I would begin a course by being very present, and then slowly disappear. A sort of vanishing act. I'd rather melt away just as I stood there, and leave a fellow more and more alone, and let him feel deserted, like a baby in a room alone.

"I know a good story, with a man's name. I don't mind using names. A fellow named Conrad

APPENDIX C

Aiken, one of our very best poets, though not one of our most read, was once told in school to interpret something from some French dramatist. He went home and got so much interested in doing it that he didn't come back to class for three weeks, but by that time he had the whole play done in verse. He was sent to the office, on the matter of cuts. He ran away on that. He came back afterwards to please an uncle, he told me. We always pleased our uncles. Is that freedom to do more than you ought to? He'd done more than a man might be asked to do in his whole college course. If a man did that for me, I'd give him A in every course."

INDEX

INDEX

INDEX